The

Holy Spirit

and

You

The Holy Spirit and You

Bernard N. Schneider

BMH Books
Winona Lake, Indiana 46590

Dedication

To the three men who greatly influenced my Christian life and ministry, I gratefully dedicate this book:

To Charles W. Mayes, beloved pastor-teacher, who led me to love the Saviour

To the late Alva J. McClain, extraordinary Bible teacher, who inspired me to love and search God's Word

To the late R. Paul Miller, faithful evangelist and soul-winner, who influenced me to love souls.

Cover photo by Dr. Lester E. Pifer

ISBN: 0-88469-049-0

COPYRIGHT 1978
BMH BOOKS
WINONA LAKE, INDIANA

Printed in U.S.A.

Foreword

Few teachings or doctrines of the Scripture prompt as many divergent opinions as that of the person of the Holy Spirit. Unfortunately, much of the material in print answers to other people's teachings rather than what the Bible says on the subject. The ability to seek out the teachings founded on the Word of God is the need of our day. So many of the phrases, such as baptism, filling and endowment mean so many things to so many different people that confusion seems to be the most prominent part of discussion.

Unfortunately, some truth is ignored because the teacher fears that he might reveal his position on a point which is the same as that of a teacher who has an opposing view of the basic doctrine of the person and work of the Holy Spirit. Thus a balanced scriptural position is lost. But the real losers are the persons who are victims of lost benefits of the unbalanced approach to truth. Either to neglect the person of the Holy Spirit or to give Him a role *not* intended is a costly mistake.

In seeking to have a Study Guide on the person and work of the Holy Spirit, we approached Dr. Bernard N. Schneider. He kindly consented to undertake this ministry. He was selected because of his person and background. He has been an active pastor through the years. His ministry has borne certain very distinct characteristics—and two of them are his faithfulness to the Scriptures and his ability to relate truth to the lives of hearers.

I believe this to be true communication and ministry. It is

possible to teach even the Bible in such a way as to make it uninviting and impractical to the person who needs truth. You will not find that to be true in this Study Guide. I think you will agree that the selection of Dr. Schneider to author *The Holy Spirit and You* proved to be a very positive one. May you be greatly benefited by this work.

Charles W. Turner
Executive Editor, BMH Books
1978

Acknowledgments

With deep appreciation I acknowledge the invaluable assistance supplied by Mary, my faithful and loving wife, in the writing of this Study Guide. She constantly encouraged me when I needed encouragement, supplied many helpful suggestions to the composition of the book, and graciously gave her patient labor in typing the final copy.

To the many friends who remembered me before the Lord in prayer while I labored over these pages, I say: THANK YOU, ONE AND ALL!

Table of Contents

Preface

In the teachings and practices of the Christian faith there are two errors which usually follow each other: namely, 1. the error of stressing a certain truth out of its intended proportion. This results in certain abuses, excesses and false teachings. 2. The error of overreacting (usually by conservative believers), which expresses itself in unduly playing down, or almost ignoring the truth that had been abused.

Church history is filled with examples of such errors. At the turn of the last century, there was a tremendous emphasis on the humanity of Christ which often resulted in the denial of His deity. The reaction among Evangelicals was a vigorous and commendable emphasis on the deity of Christ. This was good. But with this renewed emphasis on the deity of Christ, there set in a sad neglect of emphasis on the tremendously important and practical teaching of His humanity. This was unfortunate.

The practice of water baptism has somewhat the same history. For centuries there was a buildup in the stress of the importance of water baptism to the point that it was considered a saving sacrament that brought a person into the family of God. So-called "baptismal regeneration" became a widespread belief, both in Roman Catholic and some Protestant circles. The modern reaction among Evangelical teachers has been a much-needed emphasis on salvation by grace apart from human works. This is good and as it should be. But, along with this emphasis there came a down-playing of water baptism, until many believers today have not received Christian baptism since they received Christ as Saviour and Lord. This, too, is unfortunate.

Such has also been the history of the place which the Holy Spirit has received in the teaching of the Church. There was a great revival of interest in the person and work of the Spirit at the beginning of the present century, resulting in the powerful Pentecostal movement. Because this revival of interest was accompanied with some glaring abuses and errors, the unfortunate reaction among many conservatives was a lack of stress of the Holy Spirit in the teaching and preaching of the Church. At the present time there seems to be a new revival of interest, especially in the gifts of the Spirit, until in certain churches and group meetings this seems to be the main course at every gathering. This time it is called the Charismatic movement, and again there are some abuses and errors. Will we again overreact and play down or ignore the person and ministry of the Holy Spirit?

This little book is written with the purpose of calling attention to the very important place the Holy Spirit holds in the revelation of God to man which we call the Scriptures. The author claims no special qualifications for writing on this subject. He frankly admits that he has learned a great deal while spending hundreds of hours preparing for what is written in these pages.

The authority for the material in this volume is the Word of God, not the beliefs, emotions or experiences of man. The Authorized (King James) Version has been used in all quotations from Scripture except where a comparison with other translations has been made. The term "Holy Spirit" has been used by the writer instead of "Holy Ghost," except where the latter appears in quotations from the New Testament. The reason for using the word "Spirit" instead of "Ghost" is that in modern usage the word "Ghost" has become associated with spooks, phantoms and witches.

The writer has tried to avoid being too technical. His obsession in 45 years of service in the Christian ministry has been to present the great truths of the Word of God in language which everyone can understand. Hopefully he has succeeded in this study of the Holy Spirit, His person, and His ministry.

One of the aims of the Study Guides is to present sections of God's revelation to man in books that are easily read, that are teachable, and are not too bulky in size. In dealing with a major doctrine of the Scripture, such as the Holy Spirit, it is not possible to include everything on the subject in such a small volume. For that reason, certain aspects of the Holy Spirit's work had to be omitted.

The writer's fervent prayer is that the reading of these pages will lead many from the attitude of thinking of the Holy Spirit as someone in the Bible, to the place where He is recognized as the God who indwells and fills our lives; the One who is the only source of spiritual victory and joyful service; and whose main purpose in this dispensation is to produce Christ within us.

—The Author

1

John 14:1-17

The Triunity of God

I. The Meaning of the Triunity of God
   A. On the positive side, the doctrine of the triunity of God is the belief that the God of the universe exists in three persons.
   B. On the negative side, the doctrine of the triunity does not teach that there are three gods.
   C. The mystery of this doctrine

II. The Triunity of God Is Revealed in the Old Testament
   A. The oneness of God does not deny or exclude His triunity.
   B. Certain Old Testament Scriptures bear witness to the triunity of God.
   C. The triunity of God is implied in the Old Testament in the plural name of God and in the use of plural pronouns of God.

III. The Triunity of God in the New Testament
   A. Passages in which the three persons of the Godhead are named together.
   B. Scriptures where the three persons of the Godhead appear together.

Why begin this series of studies with a chapter on the triunity of God? (I prefer the term triunity over trinity.) One reason is that I have never heard a message on the triunity of God outside the seminary classroom. How many messages can you remember having heard on the subject? And yet, the triunity of God is the most basic doctrine of the Christian faith. It is the basis of man's redemption, of the deity of the Son of God, and of the personality and deity of the Holy Spirit. These vital doctrines will stand or fall with the doctrine of the triunity of God.

Liberalism is constantly attacking the doctrine of the deity of Christ as well as belief in the personality and deity of the Holy Spirit. Because of its importance, I feel constrained to introduce this series of studies on the person and work of the Holy Spirit with a brief consideration of the Biblical doctrine of the triunity of God.

I. The Meaning of the Triunity of God

A. On the positive side, the doctrine of the triunity of God is the belief that the God of the universe exists in three persons. These three persons are of one spiritual substance, of one life, of one nature, of one will, and of one equality, in such a way that the work of one is also the work of the others. Within this unity and equality there is the possibility of voluntary subordination in God's plan and operation.

In our suggested Scripture reading of John 14:1-17, all three persons appear in such a triune relationship and function. In verse 7 we find Jesus insisting: "Ye should have known my Father also: and from henceforth ye know him, and have seen him." How and when had the disciples seen God the Father? Jesus answered that question by simply stating: "He that hath seen me hath seen the Father" (v. 9). This is both great simplicity and deepest mystery.

B. On the negative side, the doctrine of the triunity does not teach that there are three gods. There is ONLY ONE GOD. "We know . . . that there is none other God but one"

(I Cor. 8:4). "The Lord our God is one Lord" (Deut. 6:4). "I am the first, and the last; and beside me there is no God" (Isa. 44:6).

C. **The mystery of this doctrine:** we worship the one and only God of heaven and earth. This God has revealed Himself to exist in three persons. This is the manner or mode of His existence. Such an existence is beyond the level of our present ability to comprehend. This is so because we have nothing like it in our experience. But then, there are many revealed facts about God that we do not understand. We cannot understand the eternity of God, because everything we know has a beginning. God has revealed these facts about Himself in His Word, and faith believes in their reality without the necessity of understanding them fully.

Although we do not need to understand the triunity of God, it is important that we know what the Word of God teaches on the subject. The purpose of this chapter is to aid in this knowledge.

II. The Triunity of God Is Revealed in the Old Testament

Nothing is taught in the New Testament concerning the triunity of God, which is not contained in the Old Testament, either in historical fact or in prophecy. For instance, the Incarnation of the Second Person, and the special advent of the Holy Spirit at Pentecost, are the fulfillments of Old Testament prophecies. At the same time, though the idea of the triunity of God is very much in evidence in the Old Testament, it does not appear very often on the surface. There is good reason for this, for one of the special assignments of God to Israel was that she was to preserve the knowledge of the Only One True God, in the midst of a world that was steeped in idolatry and polytheism. The decided emphasis of the Old Testament, therefore, is on the oneness of God. As is the case with many other important doctrines which are present in the Old Testament, the triunity of God can be fully seen only in the light of the New

Testament revelation. As has been so beautifully stated by A. W. Ingram, (as quoted) in the *International Standard Bible Encyclopedia:*

> The Old Testament, in regard to the doctrine of the Triunity is like a chamber, richly furnished, but dimly lighted. The introduction of light brings into it nothing that was not there before, but brings into clear view much that was there, but was only seen dimly or not at all.

So the New Testament brings into full view the veiled teachings of the Old Testament concerning the triunity of God.

A. The oneness of God does not deny or exclude His triunity. One of the basic revelations of God concerning Himself is the fact that He is the one and only God. "Hear, O Israel: The Lord our God is one Lord" (Deut. 6:4). Using the Hebrew names for God in this verse, it would read: "Hear, O Israel, Jehovah our Elohim is one Jehovah." This solemn declaration of the oneness of God has been used against the Christian belief in the triunity of God by the assertion that this teaches that God is singular, both in essence and in personality. If this is true, then there is something wrong with the doctrine of the triunity.

A closer examination of the word which is translated "one" in this verse, soon clears the air. The Hebrew word translated "one," is *echad.* This word is consistently used when speaking of a unity of several parts or persons. The following examples are very illuminating:

"And they [two persons, husband and wife] shall be one *[echad]* flesh" (Gen. 2:24).

"Behold, the people is one *[echad]*" (Gen. 11:6).

"And we will become one *[echad]* people" (Gen. 34:16; cf. v. 22).

"And all the people answered with one *[echad]* voice" (Exod. 24:3).

"And they shall be my people, and I will be their God: And I will give them one *[echad]* heart" (Jer. 32:38-39).

These examples are sufficient to demonstrate the fact that

the declaration "The Lord our God is one *[echad]* Lord," does not exclude the plurality of persons. The emphasis is upon the oneness of God, in the sense that there is no other God. But the one God may exist in three persons even as the "one flesh" does exist in two persons. The "one people" included many persons; the "one voice" was the assent of many persons; and the "one heart" was the spiritual unity of the people.

B. Certain Old Testament Scriptures bear witness to the triunity of God. There are a number of passages in the Old Testament which can only be understood in the light of the triunity of God, since three divine persons are presented in them. We will examine two such passages and mention additional ones for the reader's own perusal.

> The Spirit of the Lord is upon me; because the Lord hath anointed me to preach good tidings unto the meek; he hath sent me to bind up the brokenhearted, to proclaim liberty to the captives, and the opening of the prison to them that are bound (Isa. 61:1).

Three persons are mentioned in this verse; namely, (1) the Lord God, (2) the Spirit of the Lord God, and (3) the speaker, the "me," who claims to have the Spirit of the Lord upon Him, and that He is anointed to Jehovah to bring glad tidings. Since the Lord and His Spirit are mentioned by name, the question remains, who is this speaker?

The Bible is its own best interpreter, and never more so than in this case. The speaker is unquestionably the Messiah, God's Anointed, as the following facts will demonstrate: (1) The speaker claims to be anointed of God. The Hebrew title "Messiah" means "God's Anointed One" (cf. Dan. 9:25, Ps. 2:2). (2) He claims that God's Spirit is upon Him. This is repeatedly promised as part of the coming of the Messiah, as in Isaiah 11:2, "And the Spirit of the Lord shall rest upon him. . . ." The context of this verse definitely identifies the One upon whom the Spirit of God shall rest as Jesus Christ. (3) Christ Himself claimed that this passage was a prophecy that was fulfilled in Him (cf. Luke 4:16-21).

Believing firmly that the speaker in Isaiah 61:1 is identified as being the Son of God, we find three divine persons mentioned together in this Scripture; the Lord God, the Spirit of the Lord, and the Anointed of the Lord who is sent forth on a mission. Only in the light of the triunity of God can we make any sense out of this inspired verse.

> Behold my servant, whom I uphold; mine elect, in whom my soul delighteth; I have put my spirit upon him: he shall bring forth judgment to the Gentiles (Isa. 42:1).

Here we find the same three persons mentioned together. (1) The Lord (Jehovah), who is the speaker, as is clearly seen from the context. (2) Jehovah's "servant," whom the Lord calls "mine elect," and in whom His soul delights. The verses that follow (vv. 2-6) clearly identify this "servant" as the coming Messiah who will "set judgment in the earth" (v. 4), who also will be "a covenant to his people" (v. 6). (3) "My Spirit," is the Holy Spirit of God. A wonderful fulfillment of this Scripture is found in Matthew 3:16-17, which tells us of the Son of God, who,

> ... when he was baptized, went up straightway out of the water: and, lo, the heavens were opened unto him, and he saw the Spirit of God descending like a dove, and lighting upon him: And lo a voice from heaven, saying, This is my beloved Son, in whom I am well pleased.

The same three divine persons can be found together in other passages, both in the Book of Isaiah and elsewhere. I suggest a careful study of the following:

Isaiah 11:1-5. In this passage we find the Lord, "the spirit of the Lord" (who is presented here in His sevenfold fullness) and the "Branch" upon whom the Spirit shall rest, who shall smite the earth with the rod of His mouth and slay the wicked with the breath of His lips. Righteousness shall be the girdle of His loins. This can only refer to the Lord Jesus Christ and His judgment of the earth at the time of His second coming.

Isaiah 48:16. In this passage the speaker tells us He is sent forth on a mission by the Lord God and by the Spirit of God, and that speaker is the eternal I AM, who, according to the context is "the first . . . the last," who also "laid the foundation of the earth" (48:12-13).

Another interesting Scripture that adds more evidence to the presence of the doctrine of the triunity in the Old Testament, is found in Isaiah 63:7-10. Here the prophet mentions three divine persons who have a part in Israel's salvation; namely, the Lord (v. 7); the "angel of his presence who saved them" (v. 9); and "the holy spirit" (v. 10) whom Israel grieved. Such Hebrew scholars as Dr. Franz Deliztsch, Dr. C. W. E. Nagelsbach, and Dr. David L. Cooper, all regard this passage as a clear intimation of the triune existence of God.

C. The triunity of God is implied in the Old Testament in the plural name of God and in the use of plural pronouns of God. The name by which God is introduced to us in the first sentence of the Bible is the Hebrew name *Elohim* (Gen. 1:1). This is a masculine name in plural form and the same name is found almost 2,500 times in the Old Testament Scriptures. All Hebrew authorities seem to agree that this is a plural form, although there is much disagreement as to the purpose of the plural. But, whatever may be the reason, it is still in the plural. In the days of Moses and the prophets, Israel was surrounded and sometimes overcome by polytheism. They even risked their lives in the defense of the faith in the name of the one true God. I am convinced they would not have used a plural name for this God had the Holy Spirit not guided their hands as they wrote that name.

A strong testimony to the triunity of God in the Old Testament is the use of plural personal pronouns when God is quoted as speaking to, or with Himself. The first instance of this is found in the first chapter of the Bible, which fact adds to its importance. "And God [*Elohim*] said, Let *us* make man in *our* image, after *our* likeness" (Gen. 1:26).

It has been suggested that God was talking to the angels

when He said: "Let *us* make man in *our* likeness." But that explanation won't do, because the two words "image" and "likeness" are in the singular, and this means that the person or persons addressed and the speaker are of the same image and substance. The Scripture leaves no doubt about the fact that angels are created beings. They are not eternal like God. Furthermore, the whole record of creation contains not a single trace of the angels having any part in the creation. On the other hand, we are told that God created the universe (Gen. 1:1); that the Son created "all things" (Col. 1:15-19); and that the Spirit of God took part in that creation (Job 33:4; cf. 26:13).

Another similar conversation of God in which He speaks to a person or persons quite His equal, is recorded in Genesis 3:22, "And the Lord God said, Behold, the man is become as one of *us,* to know good and evil." Also note Genesis 11:7 where we read that God said: "Go to, let *us* go down, and there confound their language." The prophet Isaiah wrote (6:8): "Also I heard the voice of the Lord, saying, Whom shall I send, and who will go for *us*?"

I believe that nothing is in the Word of God by accident, but that "all scripture is given by inspiration of God," and that "holy men of God spake as they were moved by the Holy Spirit." Therefore, I am convinced that both the plural name of God, and the use of the plural pronouns by God while speaking of His work or plans, strongly imply the tri-unity of God in the Old Testament Scriptures.

III. The Triunity of God in the New Testament

A prominent Christian worker who had turned from Judaism to Christ, was asked if it were true that he was a converted Jew. "No," answered this true son of Abraham, "I am a completed Jew." This statement not only sets forth the relationship between Judaism and Christianity, but forcefully describes the relationship between the Scriptures of the Old Testament and those of the New Testament, for the New

Testament is the fulfillment of the Old. The Lord Jesus emphatically stated:

Think not that I am come to destroy the law, or the prophets: I am not come to destroy, but to fulfil. For verily I say unto you, Till heaven and earth pass, one jot or one tittle shall in no wise pass from the law, till all be fulfilled (Matt. 5:17-18).

Although the triunity of God is strongly implied in the Old Testament, especially in the promises of the coming Redeemer, it is in the New Testament where the doctrine is fully revealed. As might be expected, the strongest evidence of the triunity is presented by the Son of God, the second person of that triunity. Evidences of this triunity are very numerous in the New Testament. In fact, the triunity is taken for granted throughout the New Testament. We shall consider a few of the outstanding examples.

A. Passages in which the three persons of the Godhead are named together. The outstanding example of such passages is the Great Commission:

And Jesus came and spake unto them, saying, All power is given unto me in heaven and in earth. Go ye therefore, and teach all nations, baptizing them in the name of the Father, and of the Son, and of the Holy Ghost: Teaching them to observe all things whatsoever I have commanded you: and, lo, I am with you alway, even unto the end of the world (Matt. 28:18-20).

Christian baptism is a symbolic action which pictures the spiritual facts of the believer's deliverance from sin, his incorportion into the Body of Christ, and his entrance into the family of God. All of these spiritual facts are the work of God, received by faith. All three persons of the Godhead have a part in this work. Christ left us the ordinance of water baptism so that we might have an earthly symbol of the tremendous spiritual transaction of God. This baptism is to be in the *name* of, not in the *names* of, the Father, and of the Son, and of the Holy Spirit, indicating the unity of God and the absolute equality of the three persons. The sacred formula came from Him who declared: "That all should honour the Son, even as they honour the Father" (John 5:23). And the formula abides as an exalted and undeniable witness to the fact that the One True God exists in three persons.

The Apostle Paul, under the direction of the Holy Spirit, bears testimony to the triunity of God in one of his apostolic benedictions, as follows: "The grace of the Lord Jesus Christ, and the love of God, and the communion of the Holy Ghost, be with you all" (II Cor. 13:14). This benediction sets forth the blessing of the triune God. In the Lord Jesus Christ, the grace of God "appeared" to man. The fountain of it all is in the love of God, who "so loved the world that he gave his only begotten Son" (John 3:16). The Holy Spirit makes our fellowship with God a living reality. The fact that the order is changed here and the Lord Jesus Christ is named first, is an additional testimony to the equality of the three persons in the triune existence of the one God.

B. Scriptures where the three persons of the Godhead appear together. There are many passages in the New Testament where the three persons of the Godhead appear together in their relation to the work of redeeming man from sin. The following examples can be multiplied many times over.

> And Jesus, when he was baptized, went up straightway out of the water: and, lo, the heavens were opened unto him, and he saw the Spirit of God descending like a dove, and lighting upon him: And lo a voice from heaven, saying, This is my beloved Son, in whom I am well pleased (Matt. 3:16-17).

This was the first public appearance of Christ and all three persons of the Godhead were present—the Son, who was baptized; the Holy Spirit, who came upon the Son; and the Father, who acknowledged the Son.

> If ye love me, keep my commandments. And I will pray the Father, and he shall give you another Comforter, that he may abide with you for ever; Even the Spirit of truth.... (John 14:15-17).

> But the Comforter, which is the Holy Ghost whom the Father will send in my name, he shall teach you all things .... (John 14:26).

In both the previous passages we find Jesus speaking with perfect freedom about the relationship and harmony of purpose which exists between Him and the Father as well as the Holy Spirit. The triunity is there in such a clear and natural presentation that to doubt or deny it is to make the words of Christ either a willful blasphemy or the babbling of an unbalanced mind. The reader is invited to consider the words of John 15:26, where all three persons are mentioned again. However, there is one difference here in that Christ claimed that He would send the Spirit; whereas, a while before He said the Father would send the Spirit, "in my name" (14:26). This is a remarkable testimony to the unity of God. The work of the one person is also the work of the other two.

> And he said unto them, It is not for you to know the times or the seasons, which the Father hath put in his own power. But ye shall receive power, after that the Holy Ghost is come upon you: and ye shall be witnesses unto me. . . ." (Acts 1:7-8).

Notice how freely and naturally the risen Lord talked about the Father, the Holy Spirit, and Himself. Note, too, their relationship to each other in the overall program of God to let the world know the good news that through Christ salvation from sin is available to all.

"Elect according to the foreknowledge of God the Father, through sanctification of the Spirit, unto obedience and sprinkling of the blood of Jesus Christ" (I Peter 1:2). This is a beautiful and inspired presentation of man's salvation as provided for us by the triune God. The Father elected, according to God's foreknowledge. The Son became man and shed His blood to make this salvation possible. The Holy Spirit applies the blood of Christ to our lives in sanctification and cleansing. This work of the Spirit is here called a "sprinkling," which seems to refer to the work of applying what Christ through His blood provided.

If the contents of this chapter overwhelm you and you do not understand the triunity of God, do not be discouraged. God has not asked that we comprehend His being, He asks that we believe Him. He who created the universe by the word of His power, asks: "To whom will ye liken me, and make me equal, and compare me, that we may be like [equal]?" (Isa. 46:5). He declared: "For my thoughts are not your thoughts, neither are your ways my ways, saith the Lord. For as the heavens are higher than the earth, so are my ways higher than your ways, and my thoughts than your thoughts" (Isa. 55:8-9). Our hearts will be filled with amazement, love, and praise, when we consider that in God's eternal purpose for us, the Father has chosen, predestinated, and made us acceptable in the beloved (Eph. 1:3-6). In the Son we have redemption, forgiveness, and a wonderful inheritance (Eph. 1:7-11). The Holy Spirit has sealed us in Christ after we trusted Him as our Saviour (Eph. 1:13-14). I do not understand it all, but I surely believe God, and daily thank Him that it is true; for God cannot lie.

Questions for Discussion:

1. Why is the triunity of God basic to the Christian faith?

2. Why was the emphasis upon the oneness of God in the Old Testament Scriptures so necessary?

3. What is the significance of Christ's instruction that a believer's baptism be in the name of all three persons of the Godhead?

4. To what purpose is there a subordination of persons within the triune Godhead? Is this subordination inconsistent with the equality of those persons?

2

Acts 5:1-11; Zechariah 4:6

The Personality and Deity of the Holy Spirit

~~~~~~~~~~

THE HOLY SPIRIT IS A PERSON

I. The Holy Spirit Has All the Characteristics of Personality
- A. Intelligence
- B. A will
- C. Emotions or sensibilities
- D. Moral appreciation

II. The Activities of the Holy Spirit Demonstrate His Personality
- A. The testimony of Jesus
- B. The Scriptures

THE DEITY OF THE HOLY SPIRIT

I. The Holy Spirit Is Presented as God
- A. Matthew 28:19
- B. Genesis 1:1-2
- C. Acts 5:3-4
- D. Paul's remarkable testimony

II. The Holy Spirit Has the Attributes of God
- A. Possesses eternity
- B. Is omniscient
- C. Is omnipotent; has power
- D. Is omnipresent

III. The Holy Spirit Performs Works Which Only God Can Perform
- A. In creation
- B. Generated the humanity of Christ
- C. Regenerates
- D. Sanctifies

One of the most respected Bible teachers of recent times, Dr. John F. Walvoord, has stated in his book entitled *The Holy Spirit:*

> It is a fundamental revelation of Scripture that the Holy Spirit is a person in the same sense that God the Father is a person and the Lord Jesus Christ is a person. The Holy Spirit is presented in Scripture as having the same essential deity as the Father and the Son and is to be worshipped and adored, loved and obeyed in the same way as God. To regard the Holy Spirit in any other way is to make one guilty of blasphemy and unbelief.

In this short statement we are confronted with two important facts concerning the Holy Spirit: they are, that He is a person like the Father and the Son, and that He is as truly God as God the Father and God the Son. These facts have been the subject of constant attack and denial, both in the past and at the present time. Most present-day Liberals and Unitarians regard the Holy Spirit as the power and energy of God, but do not consider Him to be a person. There are also believers who talk of the Holy Spirit as an "It," and thus insult His person and add to the confusion.

The importance of being certain of the true nature of the Holy Spirit came to me with a jolt while reading a conclusion by Réne Pache in his book *The Person and Work of the Holy Spirit.* The conclusion reads:

> Indeed, if the Spirit were merely a power coming from above, it would be at my disposal and I could use it at will. But if the Spirit is a Person, and more than that, if He is God Himself, it is I who should be at His disposal, and love and obey Him in all things. Besides, receiving into our hearts not only a blessing, but the presence of the Almighty God is to have within us the source of all grace and of all possibility.

With this tremendous possibility facing us, let us carefully examine the Word of God and see what it has to say about the true nature of the Holy Spirit.

THE HOLY SPIRIT IS A PERSON

I. The Holy Spirit Has All the Characteristics of Personality

What constitutes personality? Many and varied are the definitions of personality, but all of them include at least three characteristics, which are: intelligence, volition, and emotion. *Intelligence* is the ability to understand and reason intelligently. *Volition* (or will) is the ability to choose and decide. *Emotion* is the ability to feel inwardly—as to love, hate, sorrow, appreciate, and so forth. A fourth characteristic which is often found in definitions of personality is that of moral appreciation, or the ability to distinguish between that which is morally right or wrong, good or evil. A person is certainly a rational and moral being.

The Holy Spirit is presented in the Scriptures as having all these characteristics in the very highest degree.

A. The Holy Spirit has intelligence. "For the Spirit *searcheth* all things, yea, the deep things of God" (I Cor. 2:10). The original word which is translated "searcheth" means to trace carefully or to track down. The same word (with the negative added) is used to tell us that God's judgments are "unsearchable" (Rom. 11:33). God's judgments often baffle us, but the Holy Spirit fully understands them, and He can reveal to us the deep things of God. We also read of "the *mind* of the Spirit" (Rom. 8:27).

B. The Holy Spirit has a will. "But all these worketh that one and the selfsame Spirit, dividing to every man severally *as he will*" (I Cor. 12:11). A careful consideration of the context (vv. 7-11) reveals the fact that the Holy Spirit bestows different gifts upon believers, *as He chooses.* What stronger proof could there be that He has both intelligence and will?

C. The emotions or sensibilities of the Holy Spirit are clearly evident. For example, we are told that He can be lied to (Acts 5:3); He can be grieved (Eph. 4:30); He may be resisted (Acts 7:51); He may also be insulted ("done despite to" Heb. 10:29). The Word speaks of "the love of the Spirit" (Rom. 15:30). We are therefore not surprised that the "fruit of the Spirit is love" (Gal. 5:22), and that "the love of God is shed abroad in our hearts by the Holy Ghost which is given unto us" (Rom. 5:5).

D. **Moral appreciation is definitely a characteristic of the Spirit.** His very name is "*Holy* Spirit." He is also called "the spirit of holiness" (Rom. 1:4). The basic meaning of "holy" and "holiness" in God's Word is that of separation from all that is evil, and dedication to that which is pleasing to God. This moral consciousness is so strong that any morally unclean or suggestive talk by the believer offends, or grieves the Spirit (Eph. 4:29-30).

II. The Activities of the Holy Spirit Demonstrate His Personality

It seems incredible that one can seriously consider the work which the Scriptures, and especially the Lord Jesus, attribute to the Holy Spirit, and still doubt or question His personality.

A. **The testimony of Jesus.** Concerning the past, Christ stated that the Spirit inspired the writers of the Old Testament Scriptures. "For David himself said *by the Holy Ghost* . . . Sit thou at my right hand, till I make thine enemies thy footstool" (Mark 12:36; cf. Ps. 110:1).

Concerning the Spirit's work during this present age, Christ promised the following:

"He shall teach you all things" (John 14:26).

"Bring all things to your remembrance" (John 14:26).

"He will reprove the world" (John 16:8).

"He will guide you into all the truth" (John 16:13).

"He will . . . speak: and he will shew you things to come" (John 16:13).

"He shall glorify me" (John 16:14).

"He shall take of mine, and shall shew it unto you" (John 16:15).

All these activities are those of an intelligent person, not of an impersonal power or influence. An impersonal power does not teach, remind, testify, reprove, guide, speak, glorify, and communicate. In this connection it is interesting to note that on His last night before His crucifixion, our Lord used the personal pronouns "him" and "himself" at least 20 times while speaking of the Holy Spirit. The Authorized and American Standard versions are in complete agreement, both in the number and in the use of these pronouns in their respective translations. This fact is a good indication that here is a fair presentation in the English language of what Christ really said.

B. Aside from Christ's own words, the Scriptures report abundant activities of the Holy Spirit which testify to His personality. Lack of space forbids a full treatment of this subject. The student will get an idea of the overwhelming testimony of Scripture to the personal activities of the Spirit by just following Him through one of the 66 books that constitute the whole Word of God.

Let us take a look into the Book of Acts. As we read through this history of the Early Church, we discover the following record:

"The Spirit gave them *utterance*" (Acts 2:4).

"The Spirit *said* unto Philip" (8:29).

"The Spirit of the Lord *caught away* Philip" (8:39).

"The churches . . . walking . . . *in the comfort of the Holy Ghost,* were multiplied" (9:31).

"The Spirit *said* unto him, Behold, three men seek thee" (10:19).

"The Holy Ghost *said,* Separate me Barnabas and Saul for the work whereunto *I have called them*" (13:2).

"So they, being *sent forth by the Holy Ghost,* departed" (13:4).

"*It seemed good to the Holy Ghost,* and to us. . . ." (15:28).

"They . . . were *forbidden of the Holy Ghost* to preach the Word in Asia" (16:6).

"But the Spirit *suffered them not*" (16:7).

"The flock, over which the Holy Ghost *hath made you overseers*" (20:28).

"And finding certain disciples ... who said to Paul *through the Spirit*" (21:4).

These quotations are self-explanatory and simply demand that the Holy Spirit of whom the Scriptures speak, is a person who acts as a person. The idea that an impersonal power or influence answers to this description is preposterous.

I want to call attenticn to one more statement in the Word of God, to add to the evidence of the personality of the Holy Spirit. In Romans, chapter 8 and verse 26, we are assured that "The Spirit itself maketh intercession for us." Can an impersonal power or influence pray for me? Can the power of God pray to God? Can anything but a person pray for us? If words have meaning, then the Holy Spirit of whom the Bible speaks, is a distinct person, not a mere power or influence of God.

THE DEITY OF THE HOLY SPIRIT

The Holy Spirit is a divine person. He is very God, one with, and equal with the Father and the Son. This means that He is equally important with the Father and the Son. The overall picture of the Scripture leaves no doubt about the Spirit's deity.

I. The Holy Spirit Is Presented as God

Reading all the references of the Scripture to the Holy Spirit certainly gives one the impression that His deity is a fact that is understood and needs no special argument. However, the following passages strongly support His deity:

A. The Great Commission: "Go ye therefore, and teach all nations, baptizing them in the name of the Father, and of the Son, and of the Holy Ghost" (Matt. 28:19). This is the name of God, given to us by the Son. This is His definition of the Godhead. In this definition, all three persons are equal, which can only mean that if one is God, the other is the same God. There is but one name. There are not three gods, but one God, who exists in three persons. The Father is God, the Son is God, the Holy Spirit is God. To conclude that one of the three is less than the other two, is doing violence to the meaning of language and is a denial of the inspiration of Scripture.

B. "In the beginning God created the heaven and the earth . . . and the Spirit of God moved upon the face of the waters" (Gen. 1:1-2). It is certainly significant that in the opening sentences of God's revelation to man, the Holy Spirit is introduced as "the Spirit of God," who is at work with God in the creation.

C. Peter told Ananias: "Ananias, why hath Satan filled thine heart to lie to the Holy Ghost? . . . thou hast not lied unto men, but unto God" (Acts 5:3-4; cf. v. 9). The very strong implication is that the Holy Spirit to whom they lied, is God.

D. Paul's remarkable testimony to the deity of the Holy Spirit. The Authorized Version renders Paul's testimony:

Now the Lord is that Spirit: and where the Spirit of the Lord is, there is liberty. But we all, with open face beholding as in a glass the glory of the Lord, are changed into the same image from glory to glory even as by the Spirit of the Lord (II Cor. 3:17-18).

The Authorized Version stands almost alone in rendering that last phrase: "even as by the Spirit of the Lord." The ARV reads: "Even as from the Lord the Spirit." Williams translates: "Since it comes from the Lord who is the Spirit." The Twentieth Century New Testament has it: "As it is given by the Lord, the Spirit." A literal rendering of the Greek would read: "Even as from Lord Spirit." We find then that the Holy Spirit is called "the Lord" twice in this passage—at the beginning of verse 17, "Now the Lord is that Spirit," and at the end of verse 18, "The Lord who is the Spirit."

II. The Holy Spirit Has the Attributes of God

This is a rich and inspiring study, but we will limit ourselves to consider only the most prominent of the divine attributes of the Spirit.

A. The Holy Spirit possesses eternity. "Christ, who through *the eternal Spirit* offered himself without spot to God" (Heb. 9:14). Dr. Chafer has pointed out that in this short statement of but 12 words, all 3 persons of the Godhead are named; "Christ," "the eternal Spirit," and "God," evidently referring to the Father. Dr. Chafer adds that, "It would be strained reasoning indeed to contend that in such a passage the identity of the Third Person is uncertain." We must not miss the significance of the fact that not only is the Spirit mentioned here as a member of the Godhead with the Son and the Father, but He is called the "eternal Spirit," and only God is eternal. All else has a beginning.

B. The Holy Spirit is omniscient. "For the Spirit searcheth all things, yea, the deep things of God. For what man knoweth the things of man, save the spirit of man which is in him? Even so the things of God knoweth no man, but the Spirit of God" (I Cor. 2:10-11). Nothing is hidden from the Holy Spirit. He understands the deepest mysteries of God, for He is God.

C. The Holy Spirit has the attribute of omnipotence; He has the power of God. "This is the word of the Lord unto Zerubbabel, saying, Not by might, nor by power, but by my spirit, saith the Lord of hosts" (Zech. 4:6). This matter of the omnipotence of the Spirit will be treated more fully under the divine works of the Holy Spirit.

D. The Holy Spirit is omnipresent. It is my understanding, based upon the study of God's Word, that only God can be present everywhere at the same time. Not even Satan has that ability. An evil spirit can indwell a human being, but only one human being at a time. However, the Holy Spirit indwells all believers at the same time. "What? know ye not that your body is the temple of the Holy Ghost which is in you" (I Cor. 6:19). That wonderful testimony of David to the omnipresence of God as recorded in Psalm 139, begins with the suggestive question: "Whither shall I go from thy spirit?" (Ps. 139:7). The Holy Spirit is present everywhere, for He is God.

He dwells within us and hears every word we utter, and knows every thought we think.

III. The Holy Spirit Performs Works Which Only God Can Perform

The activities of the Spirit are many and include those that belong only to God. While studying the activities of the Spirit, as revealed in the Word of God, a most interesting and significant fact came to me, in that I discovered that all the work that the Father does, as well as all that the Son does, is also done by the Holy Spirit. The only exceptions are those activities that demanded the incarnation of the Son, such as giving His life to accomplish man's redemption. The following are a few of the divine activities of the Holy Spirit:

A. The Holy Spirit in creation. The Spirit took part in creation in that He "moved upon the face of the waters" (Gen. 1:2). We read that "by his spirit he [God] hath garnished the heavens" (Job 26:13). The Hebrew word which is translated "garnished," speaks of adorning with beauty and splendor. The Psalmist wrote: "Thou sendest forth thy spirit, they are created" (104:30). Elihu declared: "The spirit of God hath made me, and the breath of the Almighty hath given me life" (Job 33:4). God created. The Son created (Col. 1:16). The Holy Spirit creates.

B. The Holy Spirit generated the humanity of Christ. This is one of the mysteries of the Incarnation. We know that the Father sent the Son (I John 4:14), but it was the Holy Spirit who actually generated the human body within the virgin, Mary. The Word of God is very specific and precise on the matter.

> Then said Mary unto the angel, How shall this be, seeing I know not a man? And the angel answered and said unto her, *The Holy Ghost* shall come upon thee, and the power of the Highest shall overshadow thee: therefore also that holy thing which shall be born of thee shall be called the Son of God (Luke 1:34-35).

The information given to Joseph about the situation is perhaps even more specific.

> Now the birth of Jesus Christ was on this wise: When as his mother Mary was espoused to Joseph, before they came together, she was found *with child of the Holy Ghost* . . . . The angel of the Lord appeared unto him in a dream, saying, Joseph, thou son of David, fear not to take unto thee Mary thy wife: for that which is conceived in her *is of the Holy Ghost* . . . . (Matt. 1:18-20).

The miraculous conception by the virgin Mary was the act of Almighty God, but it was accomplished through the person of the Holy Spirit. The Word of God quite simply but very definitely tells us that the person of the Holy Spirit caused the human body of the Son of God to originate within the body of Mary. This was a divine action by a person who is truly God.

C. The Holy Spirit regenerates. Speaking of the absolute necessity of being born again before any human being can see or enter the Kingdom of God, Jesus said to Nicodemus: "That which is born of the flesh is flesh; and that which is *born of the Spirit* is spirit" (John 3:6). The inspired apostle wrote: "Not by works of righteousness which we have done, but according to his mercy he saved us, by the washing of regeneration, and renewing of the Holy Ghost" (Titus 3:5). The "regeneration and renewing" by which we are saved, is the work of the Holy Spirit. The very next verse assures us that it is through Jesus Christ. Elsewhere we read that it is the work of God (John 1:13).

D. The Holy Spirit sanctifies. "Elect according to the foreknowledge of God the Father, through *sanctification of the Spirit* . . . ." (I Peter 1:2). "God hath from the beginning chosen you to salvation through *sanctification of the Spirit* . . . ." (II Thess. 2:13).

Sanctification is the work of God whereby the believer is set apart from sin unto God. This divine work has three aspects, relating to the past, the present, and the future, and is part of God's wonderful salvation through Christ. Our past sanctification took place at the time of the New Birth, when

God set us aside from sin to belong to Him. Our present sanctification is a present process whereby we are delivered from the power of sin while living· as children of God in the midst of a sinful world. The future aspect of sanctification will take place at the time of the second coming of Christ when the believer will be forever delivered from the presence of sin. Please observe that this great work of God is said to be the work of the Father (John 17:17; Jude 1). It is the work of the Son (I Cor. 1:2, 30). It is also the work of the Holy Spirit as we have seen before. The more we consider the work of the Spirit, the more we see that it is the work of God and that the three persons of the Godhead work in perfect unity and harmony, each accomplishing His particular part to complete the whole.

Conclusion:

Putting it all together, we come to the only logical conclusion, that is, the Holy Spirit of whom the Bible speaks is a person who is God and who does the work of God. And so I return to the beginning of this chapter, to the quotation taken from Réne Pache:

> Indeed, if the Spirit were merely a power coming from above, it would be at my disposal and I could use it at will. But if the Spirit is a Person, and more than that, if He is God Himself, it is I who should be at His disposal, and love and obey Him in all things. Besides, receiving into our hearts not only a blessing, but the presence of the Almighty God is to have within us the source of all grace and of all possibility.

Let us therefore not fail to yield our lives to the control of this wonderful *Paraclete!*

Questions for Discussion:

1. What Biblical evidence do we have (a) that the Holy Spirit has emotion? (b) That He has a will?
2. What significance do you find in the fact that Christ commanded Christian baptism be administered in the "*name*

of" (singular, instead of *names* of) "the Father, and of the Son, and of the Holy Spirit"?

3. Can you name at least three revealed attributes of the Holy Spirit which demand recognition of His deity?

4. Do we have scriptural evidence that our regeneration is the work of the Holy Spirit? If so, where in the New Testament is this evidence to be found?

3

Isaiah 61:1-3; Luke 4:1-21

The Holy Spirit in
His Relationship to Christ

~~~~~~~

I. The Holy Spirit Was the Author of the Virgin Birth of Christ

II. Jesus Christ Was Filled with the Spirit

III. The Holy Spirit at the Baptism of Christ

IV. Christ's Wilderness Temptation and the Holy Spirit

V. The Holy Spirit Anointed Christ for His Ministry

VI. The Holy Spirit and the Miracles of Christ

VII. The Holy Spirit Was with Christ in His Suffering and Death

VIII. The Holy Spirit Was Active in the Resurrection of Christ

IX. The Risen Christ Gave His Commands to the Apostles through the Holy Spirit

Of all the subjects dealing with the person of the Holy Spirit, the study of His relationship to Christ is the most interesting one. At the same time, it also provides some of the most perplexing problems for the human mind. Some of the greatest theologians have tried to solve these problems. It seems to me that it is futile and sometimes even dangerous to provide answers to the mysteries of God when Scripture does not supply them.

While delving into the relationship of the Spirit to Christ, the student will experience a number of surprises. The first, and perhaps the greatest of them, is the almost continuous mention of the Spirit's ministry to Christ in His earthly life. One soon discovers that the Holy Spirit was active in every phase of Christ's human life, from the conception to the ascension back to the Father's right hand. All that Christ did while on earth, He did through the Holy Spirit. This came as a surprise to me. Though I knew what the Scripture said, I had never quite put it together. I was amazed at the frequency with which the Holy Spirit is mentioned in the life of Christ.

We should clearly understand from the beginning of this study that all the ministry of the Holy Spirit in behalf of Christ had to do with the humanity of the Son. As God, the Son did not need the aid of the Spirit. However, as a man, with a true human nature, He was in constant need of the Spirit. We must never lose sight of the fact that Christ was completely God and completely man. "In him dwelleth all the fullness of the Godhead *bodily*" (Col. 2:9). In His humanity Christ was a baby who grew physically, mentally and spiritually. He was tempted, became hungry, thirsty, and weary. He wept, suffered physical pain, bled, and died. The Son of God did not become a new person in His Incarnation for He already was a person from eternity, but He did receive a new nature, a human nature. That human nature differed from ours only in that it was not affected by Adam's Fall, for it was a sinless nature. In His humanity, Christ needed the constant presence and power of the Holy Spirit to live the life and do the work for which He had become a human being. He Himself declared: "Verily, verily, I say unto you, The Son can do nothing of himself, but what he seeth the Father do" (John 5:19).

I. The Holy Spirit Was the Author of the Virgin Birth of Christ

Although this has been briefly touched upon in the preceding chapter under the divine activities of the Spirit, we need to begin this study with a consideration of this truth. As with every human being since Adam and Eve, Christ's human life began with the conception. This conception was caused by the miraculous action of the Holy Spirit. The inspired record leaves no doubt about this. Luke's account tells us what the angel said to Mary: "The Holy Ghost shall come upon thee, and the power of the Highest shall overshadow thee" (Luke 1:35).

What is meant by: "The Holy Ghost shall come upon thee"? Does it indicate some kind of physical contact? Fortunately, the Scripture holds the answer to this question. The particular wording "shall come upon thee" is used very often in the Word when speaking of a special empowering of some person by the Holy Spirit. It is found at least 15 times in the Old Testament, as in Judges 6:34, "But the Spirit of the Lord came upon Gideon." Samuel promised Saul: "And the Spirit of the Lord will come upon thee . . . ." (I Sam. 10:6). The very same phrase is used in the second chapter of Luke's Gospel where the experience of aged Simeon is reported when he saw the child Jesus in the temple: "And the Holy Ghost was upon him" (Luke 2:25). At the time of His ascension Jesus promised His disciples: "But ye shall receive power, after that *the Holy Ghost is come upon you*" (Acts 1:8). From these and other similar uses of the phrase we gather that the expression means in essence: The Holy Spirit will come into your life and take over. This is what the angel promised Mary. The Holy Spirit did come into her life, and by His divine action the new life of the baby began to be formed in her body. No suggestion of physical contact is involved.

Months later, when the perplexed husband-to-be saw that the woman to whom he was engaged to be married was with child, the angel informed him: "Joseph, thou son of David, fear not to take unto thee Mary thy wife: for that which is conceived in her *is of the Holy Ghost*" (Matt. 1:20).

At this point it is interesting to note that all three persons of the Godhead were involved in the Incarnation. God the Father was involved, for: "the Father sent the Son" (I John 4:14). Nowhere in the Scripture is the Holy Spirit called the father or the mother of Christ. Jesus spoke very often about His "Father in heaven," who would send the Holy Spirit into the world (cf. John 14:16, 26).

God the Son also had a part in the Incarnation in that He *chose* to be born into the human family. No human being ever had any choice in being born except Jesus Christ, who ever was "in the form of God . . . and *took upon him the form of a servant*" (Phil. 2:6-7). So we see that the Incarnation was the decision of the triune Godhead, which was accomplished through the agency of the Holy Spirit, the third person of the Godhead. Surely, "Great is the mystery of godliness: God was manifest in the flesh" (I Tim. 3:16).

II. Jesus Christ Was Filled with the Spirit

"And Jesus *being full of the Holy Ghost* . . . ." (Luke 4:1). Although we are not told so in any particular verse, there is good reason to believe that Christ was always filled with the Spirit in His human life, even from the time of His birth. If such was the case with John the Baptist who was "filled with the Holy Ghost, *even from his mother's womb*" (Luke 1:15), this would certainly be true of Jesus. The Word tells us: "God giveth not the Spirit by measure unto him" (John 3:34). This indicates that the Holy Spirit was present in

Christ's life in an unlimited and unhindered manner.

The Old Testament prophecies promised this unlimited work of the Spirit in Christ's life. Thus God through the prophet foretold:

> And there shall come forth a rod out of the stem of Jesse, and a Branch shall grow out of his roots: And the spirit of the Lord shall rest upon him, the spirit of wisdom and understanding, the spirit of counsel and might, the spirit of knowledge and of the fear of the Lord (Isa. 11:1-2).

Later on the same prophet quotes the coming Messiah as saying: "The Spirit of the Lord God is upon me . . . ." (Isa. 61:1). This particular promise and its fulfillment will be dealt with later on in this chapter.

Christ in His humanity was filled with the Holy Spirit. This infilling was without limitation. Add to this the fact that His humanity was not tainted, marred or limited by the results of sin. We also have good reason to believe that Jesus as a man was far above the average human being in mental capacity, in physical strength and beauty, and in winsomeness of personality and character. Although nothing is said about His physical appearance in the Word, we do read of the years of His childhood: "And the child grew, and waxed strong in spirit, filled with wisdom: and *the grace of God was upon him*" (Luke 2:40). Of the years of His youth (His teens) we read this meaningful statement: "And Jesus increased in wisdom and stature, and in favour with God and man" (Luke 2:52).

Concerning this fullness of the Spirit in the humanity of Christ, Dr. John F. Walvoord wrote:

> In contrast to the picture often drawn of Christ, His body was probably unusually strong and graceful, devoid of hereditary effects of sin as manifested in the race. . . . It is evident that the ministry of the Holy Spirit to the humanity of Christ supplied knowledge of every fact necessary to duty, to avoid sin, or to do the will of God.

III. The Holy Spirit at the Baptism of Christ

The baptism of Christ was the beginning of a new phase of

life for Him. Until then He had lived in the comparatively obscure village of Nazareth. We hear nothing of His ministry during all those years. But now the time had come for Him to begin His public ministry and to fulfill the purpose of His coming into the world: "To minister, and to give his life a ransom for many" (Matt. 20:28). To fulfill this purpose, the Holy Spirit came upon Him in a special way to supply unusual power, wisdom and guidance. From that time on He publicly manifested Himself as the promised Messiah of God. Of this special coming upon Him at the baptism, we read: "And Jesus, when he was baptized went up straightway out of the water: and, lo, the heavens were opened unto him, and he saw the Spirit of God descending like a dove and lighting upon him" (Matt. 3:16; cf. Luke 3:21-22).

IV. Christ's Wilderness Temptation and the Holy Spirit

The Saviour was "in all points tempted like as we are, yet without sin" (Heb. 4:15). The best-known series of temptation which He endured is that which followed His baptism and which began in the wilderness. The Holy Spirit was very much in evidence in that experience of the Saviour. The record reads: "And Jesus being full of the Holy Ghost returned from Jordan, and *was led by the Spirit* into the wilderness, being forty days tempted of the devil" (Luke 4:1-2).

The implication of Luke's statement is that the Holy Spirit was present with Christ in the entire experience, leading, or guiding Him through it to complete victory. This is substantiated by the information that immediately follows the temptation. "When the devil had ended the temptation, he departed from him for a season. And Jesus returned *in the power of the Spirit* into Galilee" (Luke 4:13-14). This leads me to believe that Christ did not defeat Satan by making use of His deity, but in His humanity, in which only He could be tempted and that the complete victory was by the power of the Holy Spirit. Even so is our victory over temptation found in the power of God, made available to us through the indwelling Holy Spirit.

V. The Holy Spirit Anointed Christ for His Ministry

"How God *anointed Jesus of Nazareth with the Holy Ghost* and with power: who went about doing good, and healing all that were oppressed of the devil; for God was with him" (Acts 10:38).

According to Luke, a very remarkable incident took place at the very first public message of Christ. The story is found in the fourth chapter of Luke's Gospel. Jesus had just returned from the wilderness temptation "in the power of the Spirit" (v. 14), and came back to Nazareth where He had lived for 30 years. "As was his custom," He went to the village synagogue on the Sabbath. When He volunteered to read the Scripture and bring the message of the day, the minister in charge handed Him the Book of Isaiah. Jesus opened the book to the place which to us is chapter 61, and read to the listening congregation:

The Spirit of the Lord is upon me, because he *hath anointed me* to preach the gospel to the poor; he hath sent me to heal the brokenhearted, to preach deliverance to the captives, and recovering of sight to the blind, to set at liberty them that are bruised, to preach the acceptable year of the Lord (vv. 18-19).

At that point He stopped reading, closed the book, handed it back to the minister, and as all eyes were turned upon Him, began His message with the startling announcement: "This day is this scripture fulfilled in your ears" (vv. 20-21). We do not know what more He said, but there was more, for Luke adds: "And all bare him witness, and wondered at the gracious words which proceeded from his mouth" (v. 22).

The prophet Isaiah had written down the personal proclamation of the Messiah some 700 years before Jesus came. In this proclamation the Messiah claimed to be anointed by the Spirit of God for a certain ministry. Jesus read that proclamation in His first public message (as far as we know it was the first), and then declared: "This day is this scripture fulfilled in your ears." The meaning of His declaration was plain: "I have come to fulfill this Scripture, for this speaks of me." Thus He Himself claimed to be anointed by the Holy Spirit for His ministry and mission on earth.

A quick comparison of His reading at that occasion, with the text in Isaiah from which He read, turns up the fact that He stopped reading in the middle of a sentence, for the text continues, "and the day of vengeance of our God" (cf. Isa. 61:1-3). The explanation of this is that the work of His first coming stopped where He stopped reading. The day of vengeance or the day of judgment is definitely part of His second coming. This is one of the thrilling sidelights in the study of prophetic Scriptures and their fulfillment. However, the point in our present study is the fact that for the ministry He performed in His earthly life, Jesus was anointed by the Holy Spirit.

VI. The Holy Spirit and the Miracles of Christ

Did the Holy Spirit have a part in the miracles of Christ? The answer is positive, for the Scriptures so declare. To those Jewish leaders who promoted the idea that Jesus performed His miracles through the power of the devil, Jesus declared: "But if I cast out devils by the Spirit of God, then the kingdom of God is come unto you" (Matt. 12:28). The context (vv. 24-32) reveals that attributing the work of Christ to Satan is blasphemy against the Holy Spirit. This is easily understood in the light of the fact that Christ performed the miracles in the power of the Holy Spirit.

Peter's message to Cornelius also indicates that Jesus performed at least some of His miracles by the power of the Spirit (see Acts 10:38).

VII. The Holy Spirit Was with Christ in His Suffering and Death

"How much more shall the blood of Christ, *who through the eternal Spirit offered himself without spot to God,* purge your conscience from dead works to serve the living God?" (Heb. 9:14).

As is the case with most vital Scripture passages, there is some dispute over the correct interpretation of this verse. The dispute involves the question whether this is referring to the Holy Spirit or to Christ's own spirit as a human being. But if it speaks of Christ's human spirit it would not be an eternal spirit. In the light of the fact that the Holy Spirit was present with Christ at all times, and since Christ was anointed by the Spirit for His earthly ministry and mission, I firmly believe that this is referring to the Holy Spirit, by whose enabling Christ offered Himself to God as the acceptable sin offering for the salvation of man.

The heart of the passage seems to be that Christ went to the cross voluntarily, and this He did through the Holy Spirit of God. Of this voluntary offering of Himself to God, Edwin H. Palmer wrote:

> If Jesus had gone to the cross unwillingly, sullenly, grudgingly, stoically, simply out of a feeling of necessity; and not willingly, with a perfect ardent zeal, and with faith toward the Father, no atonement could have been made. If Jesus had said: "I hate to go to the cross. I do not want to, but I suppose I have to do my duty," salvation would not have been won. No satisfaction would have been made, and no righteousness would have been available .... But, thanks to the Holy Spirit, Jesus offered a perfect sacrifice. He was not forced to die against His will, but did so voluntarily. He went to His death, knowing the consequences, but willingly, with a faith in God, and in love, trust and obedience. His attitude was perfect.

Once more I feel constrained to point out that in this most important action of the Saviour, all three persons of the Godhead had a part. It was God the Father who "hath laid on him the iniquity of us all" (Isa. 53:6; cf. v. 10). The Son openly declared:

> Therefore doth my Father love me, because *I lay down my life*, that I might take it again. No man taketh it from me, but *I lay it down of myself*. I have power to lay it down, and I have

power to take it again. This commandment have I received of my Father (John 10:17-18).

By the Holy Spirit, Christ was able in His humanity to face the awful ordeal of His death and tell the Father: "Thy will be done." The Holy Spirit was there to enable Christ to drink the cup of God's wrath upon sin, in order that we might be able to drink the cup of His salvation.

VIII. The Holy Spirit Was Active in the Resurrection of Christ

"For Christ also hath once suffered for sins, the just for the unjust, that he might bring us to God, being put to death in the flesh, but *quickened by the Spirit*" (I Peter 3:18). The Revisers have changed "by the Spirit" to read: "in the spirit," which makes it mean that Christ was made alive in His spiritual being. But, Peter is here speaking of physical death and physical resurrection, the resurrection of Christ from the grave. Christ's spirit needed not to be made alive. I believe the Authorized translation is in perfect harmony with the overall teaching of God's Word on the relationship of the Spirit to the incarnated Son, and is the correct one, meaning that Christ was quickened, or made alive, "by the Spirit."

Here too, the whole Godhead is mentioned as being active in the resurrection of Christ. We are informed that God raised up Jesus: "Whom God hath raised up, having loosed the pains of death: because it was not possible that he should be holden of it" (Acts 2:24; cf. v. 32). The Son declared: "Destroy this temple, and in three days I will raise it up," to which John quickly adds the explanation: "but he spake of the temple of his body" (John 2:19-21).

IX. The Risen Christ Gave His Commands to the Apostles through the Holy Spirit

The former treatise have I made, O Theophilus, of all that Jesus began both to do and to teach, until the day in which he was taken up, after that he *through the Holy Ghost* had given commandments unto the apostles whom he had chosen (Acts 1:1-2).

With these words Dr. Luke introduced his second treatise, addressed to his friend, Theophilus. Then he takes up his report where he had left off in his Gospel, with the ministry of Christ during the 40 days between His resurrection and ascension. This ministry was mainly taken up with the careful instruction of His apostles in the work they were to carry on in the name of Christ; beginning at Jerusalem and "unto the uttermost part of the earth." These instructions were given "through the Holy Ghost." The meaning seems to be that through the leading of the Holy Spirit, our Lord commanded and instructed His apostles in the work they were to do.

Conclusion:

We have seen how the Holy Spirit of God was closely related to all that was involved in the greatest venture of God, the redemption of man through the Incarnation of the second person of the Godhead. The Holy Spirit was present and active in this divine mission of the Son from start to finish, from the conception to the ascension. In all His humanity, Christ needed and relied upon the Holy Spirit. From this surprising discovery there comes to us the evident conclusion: If the sinless, holy Jesus constantly needed to rely upon the power and leading of the Holy Spirit, how much more do we need His power and leading! Praise be to God that this same person with all His power, is standing by, waiting on us to let Him fill our lives with His fullness.

Questions for Discussion:

1. What might Christ have meant when He said: "Verily, verily, I say unto you, The Son can do nothing of himself, but what he seeth the Father do"? (John 5:19).

2. What do we learn from the statement: "God giveth not the Spirit by measure unto him"? (John 3:34).

3. What is the significance of Jesus stopping in the middle

of a sentence while reading the Scripture for His first public message? (See Luke 4:14-21, cf. Isa. 61:1-3).

4. What evidence do we have that Christ performed at least some of His miracles by the power of the Holy Spirit?

4

Acts 2:1-21

The Coming of the
Spirit on Pentecost

I. Pentecost Had Been Promised
  A. The promise was that Christ would baptize them with the Holy Spirit.
  B. Christ spoke of the coming of the Spirit as a definite event of the future, which would occur after His own departure.
  C. The main purpose of the Spirit's coming was to glorify Christ.

II. The Fulfillment on Pentecost
  A. The miracles of Pentecost
  B. All were filled with the Holy Spirit.
  C. The greatest miracle of Pentecost was the change in the disciples.
  D. The miracle of conviction and conversion

III. The Significance of Pentecost
  A. A new dispensation began.
  B. Pentecost marked the beginning of the Body of Christ.
  C. The great significance of Pentecost is that each believer is now indwelt by the Holy Spirit of God.

When I saw the Grand Canyon for the first time, it literally took my breath away. I remember parking the car, walking over to the rim, looking across and down. Immediately, a funny feeling came to my stomach and head at the same time and I had to step back for awhile to get rid of the feeling. I understand that people have different feelings and express their reaction to the awe-inspiring sight in odd ways. I heard of one man who walked up to the rim, took one look and exclaimed: "O brother, something happened here!" That was an understatement.

This is what I feel like saying as I read the second chapter of the Book of Acts, which tells of Pentecost, of the excited disciples, of Peter's boldness, of the convicted Jews who were "pricked in their hearts," and of the 3,000 or so who received Christ as their Saviour and Lord. Something happened there! Something really did happen. The third person of the Godhead had come and had taken over, and there is nothing in the experience of mankind that can compare in spiritual power or joy with that of the Holy Spirit taking over in the lives of men and women.

I. Pentecost Had Been Promised

The special coming of the Holy Spirit at some future time had been the most important promise of Christ to His followers.

A. The promise was that Christ would baptize them with the Holy Spirit. This promise had first been given to John the Baptist by God concerning Christ. John publicly declared:

And I knew him not: but that he should be made manifest to Israel, therefore am I come baptizing with water. And John bare record, saying, I saw the Spirit descending from heaven like a dove, and it abode upon him. And I knew him not: but he that sent me to baptize with water, the same said unto me, Upon whom thou shalt see the Spirit descending, and remaining on him, the same is he which baptizeth with the Holy Ghost. And I saw, and bare record that this is the Son of God (John 1:31-34; cf. Matt. 3:11).

On the day of His ascension, Jesus referred to the promise which John the Baptist had received of God:

And, being assembled together with them, commanded them that they should not depart from Jerusalem, but wait for the promise of the Father, which, saith he, *ye have heard of me.* For John truly baptized with water; but ye shall be baptized with the Holy Ghost not many days hence (Acts 1:4-5).

The "not many days hence" turned out to be 10 days.

What is the significance of the term "baptized with the Holy Ghost"? There is scarcely another spiritual subject over which there has been as much controversy. In a later chapter we will deal with the so-called "baptism of the Spirit." (This terminology is nowhere to be found in the Word of God.) Without any intention of entering the controversy, I do present the following facts (for these are established facts) concerning the significance of the term "baptized with the Holy Ghost":

1. The one who does the "baptizing" is certainly the Lord Jesus Christ (see John 1:31-33).

2. It refers to the coming of the Holy Spirit into the lives of all believers which began on the Day of Pentecost.

3. Never once are believers asked or exhorted to seek, pray for, or in any way prepare for this baptism; it is the unconditional promise of God to all whom He has called—in other words—to all who believe (see Acts 2:38-39; cf. I Cor. 12:13).

B. Christ spoke of the coming of the Spirit as a definite event of the future, which would occur after His own departure. The student is invited to read carefully the following passages which bear overwhelming testimony to this promise:

John 14:6-17, 26
John 15:26
John 16:8, 13
Acts 1:4-5, 8-9

Earlier in His ministry, Christ described the blessed result of the Spirit's presence in the believer as follows: "If any man thirst, let him come unto me, and drink. He that believeth on me, as the scripture hath said, out of his belly [innermost life] shall flow rivers of living water." John, in recording this promise of Christ, added this significant explanation: "(But this spake he of the Spirit, which they that believe on him should receive: for *the Holy Ghost was not yet given;* because that Jesus was not yet glorified)" (John 7:37-39).

C. The main purpose of the Spirit's coming was to glorify Christ. Christ carefully described the work of the Holy Spirit, once He had come to take the Saviour's place—including convicting the world, teaching the apostles in the truth, showing them things to come and filling them with divine power. However, *the main purpose* of the Spirit's coming was to promote the Son as a person and also the Saviour. This is one of the keys to the understanding of the manifold ministry of the Spirit in this present age (of which we must not lose sight). Jesus used at least four different phrases to emphasize this purpose, as follows:

"He shall testify of me" (John 15:26).

"He will not speak of himself" (John 16:13).

"He shall glorify me" (John 16:14).

"He shall receive of mine, and shall shew it unto you . . . . he shall take of mine, and shall shew it unto you" (John 16:14-15).

The unfolding of this purpose is to be found in the Book of Acts and in the Epistles. All that is taught about the Spirit in those books bears testimony to His constant endeavor to glorify Christ, to build up the body of Christ which in turn glorifies Christ. He is the administrator of the salvation which Christ made possible through His Incarnation, culminating in His substitutionary death on the cross and His subsequent resurrection. The Holy Spirit's work during this age is to communicate and apply the salvation that Christ has wrought to human lives.

II. The Fulfillment on Pentecost

This brings us to the actual coming of the Spirit in fulfillment of the often-repeated promise of Christ. Pentecost was on the fiftieth day after Easter and ten days after the ascension of Christ to heaven. The time element suggests the question: Why did it take fifty days after the resurrection of Christ before the Spirit came? The answer is given by the inspired apostle, John, who wrote: "(But this spake he of the Spirit, which they that believe on him should receive: for the Holy Ghost was not yet given; *because that Jesus was not yet glorified*)" (John 7:39).

The Holy Spirit came to promote to man the glorified, heavenly Christ—not the earthly Christ. For 40 days after His resurrection, Christ remained on earth to instruct His disciples in "things pertaining to the kingdom of God." This instruction was "through the Holy Ghost" (Acts 1:1-3). It was after Christ was glorified, having returned to the right hand of the Father, that He sent forth the Holy Spirit to take His place and to communicate His finished work. It is also worthy of note that at the Feast of Pentecost the children of Israel flocked in great numbers to Jerusalem from all the countries where they lived. This helped greatly to spread Peter's message of the messiahship of Christ to many Jewish circles all over the world.

A. The miracles of Pentecost. As the coming into the world of the Son of God was accompanied by miracles (such as the announcement by the angel and the appearance of the star in the East), so was the coming of the Holy Spirit on Pentecost accompanied by certain signs or miracles. There was the "sound from heaven as of a rushing mighty wind" and the appearance of "cloven tongues like as of fire" (Acts 2:2-3). After the disciples were "filled with the Holy Ghost," they spoke "with other tongues, as the Spirit gave them utterance" (2:4).

What was this "speaking in other tongues"? In a later chapter we will center our attention more fully on the "gift of tongues." As far as I can determine from the report in Acts chapter 2, the speaking in other tongues on the day of Pentecost was the proclaiming of "the wonderful works of God" (v. 11) in real foreign languages by some or by all the believers present who were filled with the Spirit. The miracle was in the fact that these believers had not known those languages before. I realize that some good Bible teachers claim that even on Pentecost the speaking in tongues consisted of ecstatic utterances, not of understandable messages in a real language that was foreign to the speaker. It seems to me that the only conclusion that a sensible, open-minded reading of the report as found in Acts 2:4-11, can lead to, is that the speaking was in real languages, which were understood by visitors present from countries where those languages were spoken.

B. All were filled with the Holy Spirit (Acts 2:3). The Holy Spirit had come to take His abode within the lives of the believers who were assembled together. At that time at least, all of them were filled with the Spirit. This means that the Holy Spirit was in full control of each life. Both men and women had the same experience. Luke's statement in Acts 1:14-15 leads us to believe that about 120 persons, men and women, were involved. The Word says that the "tongues like as of fire . . . sat upon *each of them*" (2:3), and "*all* [were] filled with the Holy Ghost" (2:4).

C. The greatest miracle of Pentecost was the change in the disciples. During the days following the arrest and crucifixion of Christ, the apostles and other followers spent much of their time in hiding. They kept their doors bolted because they were afraid. Of their behavior before Pentecost we read: "Then all the disciples forsook him, and fled" (Matt. 25:56). "The doors were shut where the disciples were assembled for fear of the Jews" (John 20:19). We are all aware of the cowardice of Simon Peter who was afraid to be identified with Christ and denied that he had ever known Him. Plainly, they were all scared.

Enter Pentecost, and behold the change! Now filled with the Spirit of God, these same people displayed a holy boldness. Peter the coward had become Peter the lion. Facing those whom he had feared before, he told them:

> Ye men of Israel, hear these words; Jesus of Nazareth, a man approved of God among you by miracles and wonders and signs, which God did in the midst of you, as ye yourselves also know: Him, being delivered by the determinate counsel and foreknowledge of God, ye have taken and by wicked hands have crucified and slain: Whom God hath raised up, having loosed the pains of death: because it was not possible that he should be holden of it .... Therefore let all the house of Israel know assuredly, that God hath made that same Jesus, whom ye have crucified, both Lord and Christ (Acts 2:22-24, 36).

Something tremendous had happened to that man. Evidently the promise of Christ: "Ye shall receive power, after that the Holy Ghost is come upon you" (Acts 1:8) had been gloriously fulfilled.

D. The miracle of conviction and conversion. "Now when they heard this, they were pricked in their heart, and said unto Peter and the rest of the apostles, Men and brethren, what shall we do?" (Acts 2:37).

The promise of Christ had been that when the Spirit came, He would "reprove the world of sin, and of righteousness, and of judgment" (John 16:8). This work of the Spirit was very much in evidence on the day He came. The Jews who heard the message of Peter as he presented Christ as the risen Redeemer, were "pricked in their hearts." The message went straight to the heart. The Holy Spirit brought this conviction, and the listeners wanted to know what they ought to do. This was a miracle, brought on by the working of the Spirit. Yes, Peter was a good preacher that day, but not *that* good. I have seen the same power of the Holy Spirit doing the same thing in the hearts of some of the toughest of men, and I knew that only the Spirit could produce such conviction.

"Then they that gladly received his word [Peter's message]

were baptized: and the same day there were added unto them about three thousand souls" (Acts 2:41). This was the beginning of the miracle of people turning to Christ upon hearing the message of God's salvation and being convicted by the Holy Spirit. The results that followed in the days immediately after Pentecost are truly amazing. Consider these reports: "About three thousand souls" (2:41). "The Lord added to the church daily such as should be saved" (2:47). "Howbeit many of them which heard the word believed; and the number of the men was about five thousand" (Acts 4:4). "And believers were the more added to the Lord, multitudes both of men and women" (Acts 5:14). "And the number of the disciples multiplied in Jerusalem greatly; and a great company of the priests were obedient to the faith" (Acts 6:7).

III. The Significance of Pentecost

A. A new dispensation began. The coming of the Holy Spirit into the world to be the administrator of the work of Christ was the commencement of a completely new age or dispensation in God's dealings with man. This age is known among believers by different names, such as the Church age, the age of Grace and the age or dispensation of the Spirit. In this age the Holy Spirit is permanently living in, and working through the lives of believers.

This age began on Pentecost and will close with the Spirit's departure at the time of "our gathering together unto him" (II Thess. 2:1), commonly known among us as the Rapture of the Church. This departure of the Holy Spirit is indicated by the apostle's inspired explanation: "For the mystery of iniquity doth already work: only he who now letteth will let, until he be taken out of the way. And then shall that Wicked be revealed . . . ." (II Thess. 2:7-8). This reading from the Authorized Version is somewhat difficult for us. The ASV translates: "Only there is one that restraineth now, until he be taken out of the way."

The Holy Spirit, working through the lives of believers, is

restraining the complete takeover of evil in the world. When the Spirit will depart (with the Body of Christ), this restraint will be gone and the Antichrist will take over in the power of Satan.

There are certain facts about this present age which we should know and keep in mind, in order to better understand God's plan for man: namely,

1. In this age God is calling out of the world, from among both Jews and Gentiles, a people for His name. 2. In this age Israel is set aside temporarily as far as the divine purpose for that people is concerned. 3. This present age (from Pentecost to the return of Christ) is not foretold or foreseen in God's revelation to man in the Old Testament Scriptures.

B. Pentecost marked the beginning of the Body of Christ. This is the purpose of God for this age. He is calling out of this world a people who make up the true Church which is the Body of Christ whereof He is the Head.

> For by one Spirit are we all baptized into one body, whether we be Jews or Gentiles, whether we be bond or free; and have been all made to drink into one Spirit. Now ye are the body of Christ, and members in particular (I Cor. 12:13, 27; cf. Eph. 4:11-16).

The forming of that Body began with the 130 believers on the Day of Pentecost when the Spirit came to indwell them. Before the day was over about 3,000 were added. The record, as it stands in our Bible reads: "And the same day there were added unto them about three thousand souls" (Acts 2:41). If you take a close look at the verse you will notice that the two words: "unto them" are in italics, which means that they are not found in the original, but are added by the translators. A look at Acts 5:14 reveals the fact that "believers were the more *added to the Lord,* multitudes both of men and women." The words "to the Lord" are not in italics because they are present in the original. Believers are being added to the local congregation but so are some added who are not born again. This is because *we* add members to the congregation. But only the Holy Spirit can add people to the Lord, and He adds only those who are born again.

C. The great significance of Pentecost is that each believer is now indwelt by the Holy Spirit of God. "Now if any man have not the Spirit of Christ, he is none of his" (Rom. 8:9). "Know ye not that ye are the temple of God, and that the Spirit of God dwelleth in you?" (I Cor. 3:16). The third person of the Godhead dwells within us. Think of the possibilities! Think of the responsibilities!

The following did not happen to me, but it really did happen to a pastor. This man was the pastor of a congregation in a small town, some distance from a large city. One Tuesday morning he drove to the city to make purchases. When he got to the checkout counter with his basket and reached in his hip pocket to pay for his purchases, he discovered to his chagrin that the billfold was not there. We can imagine his embarrassment! He concluded that it was still in the suit which he had worn the evening before. There was nothing to do but to go home empty-handed. He could not even buy a cup of coffee. His credit cards were also in that billfold. He drove home very carefully and five miles an hour slower than his usual speed because his driver's license was in the absent billfold. Arriving home, he went straight to the bedroom to get that billfold. But, when he dug into the pockets of the other trousers, the billfold was not there. It was not to be found anywhere in the other suit. Fear struck his heart. Had he lost the pocketbook? Almost automatically he searched every pocket of the suit he was wearing—and there, in his right coat pocket was the billfold. He had it with him all the time and could have made all the planned purchases. He had been helpless, poor and embarrassed because he did not know what he had with him.

Is not this true of many believers who are powerless and joyless in their Christian lives? And all the time the Holy Spirit, the source of all spiritual victory, joy and blessing, is dwelling within, waiting to be trusted with our lives. Jesus promised: "Ye shall receive power, after that the Holy Ghost is come upon you." The "power" was sufficient to change a scared, hiding Peter into a fearless dynamo for Christ.

Questions for Discussion:

1. What purpose did the miracles which accompanied the coming of the Holy Spirit serve?

2. Can you name the main purpose of the Holy Spirit in this present age?

3. What do you consider to be the greatest miracle that happened on the Day of Pentecost?

4. Does the Word of God teach that each believer is indwelt by the Holy Spirit? Where in the New Testament can we find this?

5

John 16:1-15; I Corinthians 2:14

The Holy Spirit
and the World

I. The Threefold Conviction of the Spirit in the World
   (John 16:6-11)
   A. "He will reprove the world of sin .... Of sin, because they
      believe not on me" (John 16:8-9).
   B. Conviction of righteousness "because I go to my Father, and
      ye see me no more" (cf. John 16:8 and v. 10).
   C. The Holy Spirit will convict the world "of judgment .... be-
      cause the prince of this world is judged" (John 16:8, 11).
   D. The Holy Spirit works through believers in His threefold con-
      viction of the world.
   E. The conviction of the Holy Spirit is supernatural conviction.

II. The Restraining Work of the Holy Spirit in the World

The subject of the Holy Spirit and His work in the world should be one of the most practical studies for believers today.

The "world" of which Jesus spoke is the *kosmos,* the great arrangement of world order which man likes to call CIVILIZATION. Of this world, Satan is the "prince" or chief. He is the world's spiritual mastermind and directs its course. This world has no room for the holy and righteous God of the universe and crucified the Son whom God sent to bring salvation to mankind. This world is made up of people, more of them today than ever before.

Jesus said two things about the Holy Spirit and the world. He said that the world cannot receive the Spirit, and that the Spirit would convict the world of sin, and of righteousness, and of judgment. What can this mean? If we have the idea that Jesus meant that the Holy Spirit is going about on His own in the unregenerated world, convicting the unsaved of being sinners and of being headed for judgment, we are mistaken, for that just isn't the case. Nor is that what the New Testament teaches. There are millions of people today who haven't even heard of Jesus Christ, and since the sin of which the Spirit is to convict the world is that of not believing in Christ, we may well exclaim with Paul: "How shall they believe in him of whom they have not heard?" (Rom. 10:14). Evidently, there must be more involved. There is, and that is where believers come in.

There is a second work which the Holy Spirit is doing in the world, and that is His restraining of evil. This work also involves the believer, and we will deal with it briefly at the close of this chapter.

I. The Threefold Conviction of the Spirit in the World (John 16:6-11)

The first thing that I notice about this promise of Christ is that the Holy Spirit's work of convicting the world was to be of special advantage to the followers of Christ. The apostles were so very sad because the Lord kept talking about leaving them (see 16:1-6). But Jesus told them, "It is expedient for you that I go away." It was to their advantage, for their benefit, "for," He continued, "If I go not away, the Comforter will not come unto you; but if I depart, I will send him unto you. And when he is come, he will reprove the world of sin, and of righteousness, and of judgment."

Christ was about to send His disciples out into the hostile world to preach the Gospel to every creature. What chance did they have of ever getting off the ground with it? Obviously none. But with the Holy Spirit doing the inside work while they did the outside work, there would be great success. The first Christian witness on Pentecost demonstrated this as 3,000 responded by receiving Christ as Saviour and Lord of their lives. This convicting work of the Holy Spirit is definitely related to believers. It is a real boon to them. More of this later.

A. "He will reprove the world of sin . . . . Of sin, because they believe not on me" (John 16:8-9). The Greek word which is translated "reprove" in the Authorized Version, is *elegcho,* and is found seventeen times in the Greek text of the New Testament. Five times it is translated in our Bible by the word "convince" (cf. Titus 1:9). Five times it is translated "rebuke," as in Titus 1:13, and in five instances it is translated "reprove" as in John 16:8 (cf. John 3:20). Once it is translated "convict," as follows: "And they which heard it, being *convicted* by their own conscience . . . ." (John 8:9). According to some Greek scholars, the Greek word *elegcho* carries the meaning of presenting evidence which condemns.

We note that the Spirit convicts the world of sin, not sins. The particular sin of which He proves the world guilty is that of unbelief regarding the Son of God. A helpful paraphrase might read: "When the Holy Spirit is come, He will convict the world of the reality of sin as *embodied* in the fact that the world has rejected me." According to Samuel Rideout, a preacher stated from the pulpit of a certain church on Sunday morning: "If virtue were to appear upon the earth incarnate, ravished by her beauty, men would fall down and worship her." Whereupon a man of God on the same day in the evening, from the same pulpit, stated: "Virtue incarnated did come to earth, and men's cry was 'Away with him, crucify him.'"

Most certainly, the sin that dooms man finally is rejection of Christ. Jesus had stated this fact on other occasions. To Nicodemus, He said:

> For God so loved the world, that he gave his only begotten Son, that whosoever believeth in him should not perish, but have everlasting life. For God sent not his Son into the world to condemn the world; but that the world through him might be saved. He that believeth on him is not condemned: but he that believeth not is condemned already, because he hath not believed in the name of the only begotten Son of God. And *this* is the condemnation, that light is come into the world, and men loved darkness rather than light, because their deeds were evil (John 3:16-19).

All the sinfulness of sin was displayed in the betrayal, mock trial, and crucifixion of the Son of God. On the Day of Pentecost, Peter charged his hearers with that sin, and the Holy Spirit used that presentation to bring people face to face with their sinfulness until they "were pricked in their heart, and said . . . what shall we do?" (Acts 2:37). The great need of the church in her work of evangelizing is to present the reality of sin. The world does not believe in the reality of sin today. The great tragedy is that the subjects of sin and its consequence, eternal punishment in hell, are more and more conspicuous by their absence from the curriculum of the preaching and teaching of the church. What is the reason for this neglect? Could it be that we are afraid that the world won't like these subjects? The world has never liked them. But this is the message that the Spirit of God has come to back up with conviction.

I do not remember a conversion that was lasting and real without the person experiencing a real conviction of sin. We are not going to turn ourselves over to a physician for serious surgery unless we are first convinced that it is absolutely necessary. Neither does a person turn himself over to God unless he is convinced of its absolute necessity. Whether in the official proclamation of the message of evangelism, or in a personal endeavor to win an individual to Christ, or while counseling a burdened soul; there must be an emphasis on the reality of sin. This is the basis of man's need of the Saviour. We need to make it plain that man is a guilty sinner, that the only remedy for sin is in Jesus Christ, and that the worst sin is to reject or ignore this Saviour. We need not be afraid to speak of the reality of sin because the Holy Spirit of God will back us up.

B. Conviction of righteousness "because I go to my Father, and ye see me no more" (cf. John 16:8 and v. 10). The Holy Spirit convicts the world of the reality of righteousness, and the great proof of the reality of righteousness is the resurrection of Christ and His acceptance at the right hand of the Father.

In reading through a number of commentaries and books on theology that deal with the subject of the Holy Spirit's function of convicting the world of righteousness, I found quite a variety of ideas as to the meaning of righteousness in verse 8. About half of the writers suggest that Christ is here speaking of imputed righteousness, that is, the righteousness with which God credits a person who receives Christ as Saviour. Others believe that Christ was speaking of His own righteousness. I am sure in my mind that both views are right, for, there is only one righteousness, and that is perfect righteousness. There is only one straight line—and that is a perfectly straight line—but there are thousands of different crooked lines. There are also a number of different names for sin in the Bible—such as evil, iniquity, transgression, and so on. That is because there are different kinds of sin. But, there is only one word for righteousness, because there is only one righteousness, and that is the righteousness of God. "God is light, and in him is no darkness at all" (I John 1:5). No man or woman is going to enter heaven without having this same righteousness. The Biblical facts concerning righteousness are as follows:

God is absolutely righteous in His character and in all His acts. This righteous God *requires* righteousness of man. But no human being is righteous, as the Word of God says: "There is none righteous, no, not one" (Rom. 3:10). "For all have sinned, and come short of the glory of God" (Rom. 3:23). The righteous God, in His love for man, sent the Son of God into this world to do something about man's need and lack of righteousness. The Son came, lived a righteous life, gave His life as a perfect sacrifice for man's sin, was raised from the grave and was seated at the right hand of God, thus demonstrating His righteousness. And now God asks man to trust in His Son as Saviour from sin, in order that Christ's righteousness can be credited to man. God "made him to be sin for us, who knew no sin; that we might be made the righteousness of God in him" (II Cor. 5:21). See also Romans 3:21-22. That is why "There is therefore now no condemnation to them which are in Christ Jesus . . . ." (Rom. 8:1).

The Holy Spirit convicts of the reality of righteousness—the righteousness which is found in God, the righteousness which God requires, and the righteousness which God imputes or credits to the sinner when he places his trust in Christ as his own Saviour. To put it another way, Christ is our righteousness. "But of him [of God] are ye in Christ Jesus, who of God is made unto us wisdom, and *righteousness,* and sanctification, and redemption" (I Cor. 1:30).

The reality of righteousness is one of the basics of all true evangelism. Man needs to know that there is such a thing as righteousness, as demonstrated by Christ. Man also needs to know that God requires this righteousness of man, that man has no righteousness, and that God has provided it for him in Jesus Christ. This is truth that the Holy Spirit will back up with supernatural conviction. The writer has faced many a person with the fact that God sees you either in your sin or in His Son.

C. **The Holy Spirit will convict the world "of judgment . . . . because the prince of this world is judged" (John 16:8, 11).** The Spirit convicts the world of the reality of judgment. On Calvary's cross, Satan's total defeat was accomplished. There the "prince of this world" was judged. A few days previously Jesus announced: "Now is the judgment of this world: now shall the prince of this world be cast out" (John 12:31). In the wisdom of God, Satan is still permitted to pursue his course, but he has been judged and his final doom is certain. The time will come when the sentence will be carried out. Having been shown the end of Satan, John wrote: "And the devil that deceived them was cast into the lake of fire and brimstone, where the beast and the false prophet are, and shall be tormented day and night for ever and ever" (Rev. 20:10).

The judgment of the world is also certain. Its chief has already been judged and the world's judgment is sure to follow. The resurrection of Christ is God's solemn guarantee that the world's judgment will be carried out. "Because he [God] hath appointed a day, in the which he will judge the world in righteousness by that man whom he hath ordained; whereof he *hath given assurance unto all men,* in that he hath raised him from the dead" (Acts 17:31). The only way to escape that judgment is to be saved out of this world. Jesus said: "Verily, verily, I say unto you, He that heareth my word, and believeth on him that sent me, hath everlasting life, and shall not come into condemnation [judgment] ; but is passed from death unto life" (John 5:24).

The world today likes to make light of judgment, but the Holy Spirit will back up the presentation of the reality and certainty of the world's judgment, and the safety from that judgment that is found in Christ.

D. **The Holy Spirit works through believers in His three-fold conviction of the world.** Jesus made it plain that the unsaved cannot receive the Spirit of God (see John 14:17). We are also assured that "the natural man receiveth not the things of the Spirit of God: for they are foolishness unto him: neither can he know them, because they are spiritually discerned" (I Cor. 2:14).

One of the basic truths of the New Testament is that in all His work of communicating the message of salvation to lost men and women, the Holy Spirit depends upon, and works only through believers. He works through the lives they live and through their oral or written witness of Christ. This is also true of His work of conviction. Consider the documented history of the Early Church as found in the Book of Acts: The Spirit worked through the apostles on Pentecost. He worked through Philip in Samaria, and then sent him into the desert to witness to one man, the treasurer of Ethiopia. A very reluctant Peter had to tell Cornelius and his household the way of salvation. The Lord sent Ananias to deal with Saul in Damascus. No doubt Saul was under deep conviction for some time because of the witness he heard from Stephen, and from the testimony of Stephen's behavior when they stoned him to death. Saul fought that conviction, as is indicated by our Lord's statement: "It is hard for thee to kick against the pricks" (Acts 9:5). The entire Book of Acts is the story of how God used believers to witness to unbelievers, the Holy Spirit backing them up by bringing conviction. The ones witnessed to did not always respond favorably, but they were usually under deep conviction—as is indicated by the fury of the mob that stoned Stephen, or by the trembling of Felix, or the response of Agrippa: "Almost thou persuadest me to be a Christian" (Acts 26:28). Believers were faithful in those days to witness for Christ, and the Holy Spirit was faithful to bring conviction.

This plan of God has not changed since those days. Missionaries still have to take the message of God's salvation to distant places. The Holy Spirit works through them and in due time the miracle of conversion occurs. A congregation of believers has a burden for the lost and individuals begin a Spirit-led witness. The result is a heaven-sent revival.

I would like to share my own testimony at this point. Forty-six years ago I lived in Southern California. I was living a godless and selfish life, giving God no thought. I had never been inside a Protestant church. A lady who lived nearby went to her pastor one Sunday evening and confessed that although she had been a Christian for 45 years, she had never tried to win a soul to Christ. The two prayed together and the lady promised the Lord that she would witness to the first person He would lead her way. The Lord gave her a burden for me and on Monday evening she witnessed to me. I did not know her and did not like it. And though the Lord used others later on to explain the salvation of the Lord more fully, I know that without that woman's contact I might never have been saved. She did not know the rules of successful witnessing. She had no experience in it. The "Four Spiritual Laws" were not yet written. But she obeyed the Lord, the Holy Spirit did the inside work, and here I am!

E. The conviction of the Holy Spirit is supernatural conviction. This is obvious, since it is the work of the Holy Spirit of God. But we sometimes seem to forget this, and try to do the Spirit's work, or rely upon our own ability to produce conviction. There is an undue emphasis and reliance upon the use of human psychology among some Christian workers today. But psychology can never bring a soul to Christ. Only the Holy Spirit can do that. Psychology in Christian work is like education in general—it can be a great aid in communicating the message of the Lord and in teaching God's Word. But, when psychology or education is relied upon to produce spiritual results, it becomes a curse instead of a blessing. Sometimes actual trickery is used by evangelists to get decisions, but all such efforts are of the flesh, and God cannot use flesh. The only one who can produce spiritual conviction is the Holy Spirit. The only message which He can use is the Word of God. Everything else will fail. The Apostle Paul said:

"And I, brethren, when I came to you, came not with excellency of speech or of wisdom, declaring unto you the testimony of God. For I determined not to know any thing among you, save Jesus Christ, and him crucified" (I Cor. 2:1-2). Oh, that every pastor, missionary, counselor, and teacher might have the same ambition as did Paul, who must have been one of the best-educated men of his time.

Many are the memories of witnessing the supernatural conviction of the Holy Spirit. I well remember how a man fought this conviction. His family suffered from it. But one Sunday morning he was present and when the invitation was given at the close of the message, he came stumbling down the side aisle. His face was drained of color and his body was reeling. As he turned the corner at the end of the aisle, he fell forward and I caught him as he fell. Then the whole congregation heard him sob out, "I just give up." That was the work of the Holy Spirit. When the Spirit was at work, I have seen tears of conviction while the opening hymn was being sung in a service. At such times I stood by in awe, with shivers going up and down my spine, as the evidence of the working of the Holy Spirit was seen. I remember a couple coming to our door after the evening service, begging us with tears to call the congregation back together so these two who were under conviction could make public confession of Christ as their Saviour. I know that this was the work of the Spirit. He still convicts of sin, and of righteousness, and of judgment.

II. The Restraining Work of the Holy Spirit in the World

And now ye know what withholdeth that he [the Antichrist] might be revealed in his time. For the mystery of iniquity doth already work: only he who now letteth [restraineth] will let [continue to restrain], until he be taken out of the way. And then shall that Wicked be revealed . . . . (II Thess. 2:6-8).

The context shows that Paul was speaking of the return of Christ. The believers in Thessalonica had been bothered by teachers who said that Christ had already come. Paul was showing them that before the coming of Christ in glory there would be a great falling away from the faith, and the Antichrist would appear with his evil ways. "The mystery of iniquity is already at work" wrote the inspired apostle. "But there is one who still restrains the evil, and he will continue to restrain until He is taken out of the way. Then the Lawless One will take over" (II Thess. 2:6-8 lit. trans.).

The one who restrains can be none other than the Holy Spirit. He restrains the wickedness of the world so that it is not as bad as it can be, and as it will be when He is gone. He will leave with the Body of Christ just before the Antichrist will appear to take over in the world.

This restraining of evil by the Holy Spirit is also accomplished through believers. Jesus said: "Ye are the salt of the earth . . . . Ye are the light of the world" (Matt. 5:13-14). Weak as it may seem at times, there is still a mighty influence of the Holy Spirit upon the world through the lives and teaching of God's people. It is still restraining the worst that is in man. True, evil is getting more bold every day. Unnatural passions that were once publicly loathed, are now parading in the open. But when all restraint will be gone, it will be far worse. For further information, read the Book of Revelation!

These lines are being written (July 1977) while the papers are still full of the stories about the great blackout of New York City, where seven million people were suddenly without light. When this happened, hordes of people came out to destroy and to loot, throwing bricks through windows, gutting stores, carrying off anything from liquor to television sets. Three thousand people were arrested and eighty policemen were injured. The streets were littered with debris. When the lights went out, iniquity took over.

We are seeing a gradual, but constant takeover of evil in the world today. It can be seen in the ever-increasing use of profanity and obscene expressions in public entertainment and in books. But the worst is still being held back. The Holy Spirit is still here to restrain through the lives and testimonies of His people. One of these days God will forsake the earth and for the seven years of the Tribulation period, evil will be ruling without the restraining hand of God. I am glad that I won't be around when that happens.

Questions for Discussion:

1. What was it that brought our need of salvation to our attention? (Opportunity for testimonies on this question may prove helpful).

2. Why is the refusal to believe in Christ the sin that dooms the soul?

3. What guarantee has God given that the world will finally be judged?

6

John 3:1-21

The Holy Spirit
and the New Birth

I. **The Meaning of the New Birth**
   A. A definition: A new birth is the supernatural act of God whereby a person passes from the state of spiritual death to that of spiritual life.
   B. The new birth is the act of God.
   C. The new birth is accomplished through the Holy Spirit.

II. **The Necessity for the New Birth**
   A. The new birth is necessary because a person is not a child of God without it.
   B. Man must be born again because he has the wrong nature for God's kingdom.
   C. Man must be born again because he is a lost and condemned sinner.

III. **The Holy Spirit's Part in the New Birth**
   A. The Spirit imparts new life.
   B. The Holy Spirit comes to indwell the believer.
   C. The believer is sealed with the Holy Spirit.
   D. The believer is baptized with (or in) the Spirit and is placed in vital union with Christ.
   E. The Holy Spirit becomes the believer's unlimited resource for a successful Christian life.

"Born again" has recently become a catch phrase in our nation and is being used by reporters, writers, and news commentators as perhaps never before. With some, it is a phrase which signifies a revival of religious interest in general. Others use it to speak of the Charismatic movement in particular. The use of the term "born again" by our president, Mr. Carter, and by others who are much in the public's eye, has given the words some respectability. However, in many instances the words are used in the world with considerable derision, which is sometimes veiled and sometimes quite open—as though it were a pretended something that really fools no one who is in his right mind. It still remains true that very few (if any) outside of those who have actually experienced the new birth, have the slightest idea what it really means to be born again.

According to our Lord Jesus Christ, the greatest need of man is to be born again. The greatest thing by far that can happen to a person is to be born again. The subject of the new birth is therefore of such vital importance that one should never trifle with it nor take it lightly. In our present study we are going to consider the new birth—what it is, why it is so necessary, and how it is received, with particular attention given to the part that the Holy Spirit has in it all.

I. The Meaning of the New Birth

Verily, verily, I say unto thee, Except a man be born again, he cannot see the kingdom of God . . . . Except a man be born of water and of the Spirit, he cannot enter into the kingdom of God . . . . Marvel not that I said unto thee, Ye must be born again (John 3:3, 5, 7).

A. A definition: The new birth is the supernatural act of God whereby a person passes from the state of spiritual death to that of spiritual life. Through this act of God, man receives eternal life and becomes a child of God. This action of God is made possible through the substitutionary death of the Son and is communicated to man by the Holy Spirit.

B. The new birth is the act of God.

> He came unto his own, and his own received him not. But as many as received him, to them gave he power to become the sons of God, even to them that believe on his name: Which were *born*, not of blood, nor of the will of the flesh, nor of the will of man, but *of God* (John 1:11-13).

Born of God! This is entirely the work of God.

A great deal of misunderstanding and confusion will be avoided in the teaching and study of God's Word, if we make a clear distinction between what God tells or commands man to do, and what God has promised to do. For instance, man is commanded to repent and to believe. This is *our* responsibility. Of course, even in this we need the help of the Holy Spirit to enlighten and convict us, but it is our responsibility to respond to the light and the conviction that the Spirit brings. The new birth on the other hand, is the complete work of God. In the First Epistle of John, the words "born of God" appear six times. Any human effort, therefore, in securing the new birth or aid in securing it is utter folly and constitutes an insult to God.

C. The new birth is accomplished through the Holy Spirit.

"Except a man be born of water and of the Spirit, he cannot enter into the kingdom of God. That which is born of the flesh is flesh; and that which is born of the Spirit is spirit . . . . So is every one that is born of the Spirit" (John 3:5-6, 8). "Not by works of righteousness which we have done, but according to his mercy he saved us, by the washing of regeneration, and renewing of the *Holy Ghost*" (Titus 3:5).

A great deal of controversy has surrounded the interpretation of the words of Jesus: "born of water and of the Spirit" (John 3:5). There is no question about the meaning of "Spirit," for it can only refer to the Holy Spirit. But what is meant by "born of water"? Some have made it to mean water baptism, and have thus aided Satan in the use of one of his most effective counterfeits of the true Gospel, the counterfeit of adding something to, or substituting something for the finished work of Christ as the basis of man's salvation.

Water is used in both the Old and New Testaments when speaking of the cleansing work of the Holy Spirit through the Word of God. The words of Jesus (John 3:10) suggest that Nicodemus, who was a teacher of Old Testament Scripture, should have known the meaning of "born again." It appears that our Lord had in mind such declarations as found in Ezekiel 36:25-27:

> Then will I sprinkle clean water upon you, and ye shall be clean: from all your filthiness, and from all your idols, will I cleanse you. A new heart also will I give you, and a new spirit will I put within you: and I will take away the stony heart out of your flesh, and I will give you a heart of flesh.

The Psalmist declared: "Wherewithal shall a young man cleanse his way? by taking heed thereto *according to thy word*" (Ps. 119:9). In the New Testament we find that water is used to emphasize the cleansing power of the Word of God when applied by the Holy Spirit. "Now ye are clean through the word which I have spoken unto you" (John 15:3). "That he might sanctify and cleanse it with the *washing of water by the word*" (Eph. 5:26). Furthermore, the Word of God is clearly identified as being used by God in accomplishing the new birth. "Of his own will *begat he us with the word of truth*" (James 1:18). "Being born again, not of corruptible seed, but of incorruptible, *by the word of God* which liveth and abideth for ever . . . . And this is the word which by the gospel is preached unto you" (I Peter 1:23, 25).

Because of this convincing evidence, I believe the "water" in John 3:5 denotes the Word of God which is used by the Holy Spirit to bring conviction of sin and understanding of God's salvation through Christ—thus preparing a person to believe in the Lord Jesus for salvation.

II. The Necessity for the New Birth

No subject in all the Saviour's teaching is stated more emphatically than the necessity of the new birth. He stated that unless a person is born again, he "cannot see the kingdom of God," and he "cannot enter into the kingdom of God" (John 3:3, 5). The "kingdom of God" here indicates the company of God's redeemed, or the family of God—those who have become His children (cf. John 1:11-13). Twice Christ used the words "verily, verily" when speaking about this necessity, thus indicating the importance of His pronouncement. Then He followed that by declaring: "Marvel not that I said unto thee, Ye must be born again" (John 3:7).

Why this absolute necessity? Although a full discussion of this question is not intended here, I present the following Biblical facts, almost all of which are found right here in the words of Christ to Nicodemus.

A. The new birth is necessary because a person is not a child of God without it. "But as many as received him, to them gave he power *to become* the sons [children] of God, even to them that believe on his name" (John 1:12). If we become children of God through faith in Christ Jesus, it can only mean that until we are born of God (v. 13), we are not children of God. This is the basic truth behind the necessity of the new birth. This is where we must begin in our approach to win people to Christ at home or on any mission field in the world. We must accept and be convinced of the unalterable fact that until a person is born again, is born of God, he is not and never can be a child of God.

Elsewhere in the New Testament the same truth is emphasized by declaring that without the new birth, man is "dead in trespasses and sins" (Eph. 2:1, cf. v. 5; Col. 2:13). Through the new birth a person receives new life, eternal life, and becomes spiritually alive.

B. Man must be born again because he has the wrong nature for God's kingdom. Jesus said it like this: "That which is born of the flesh is flesh" (John 3:6). In our physical birth we received a fallen, sinful human nature that is blind and opposed to the things of God. It is born of the flesh and can never rise higher than the flesh. In fact, that nature is totally depraved and cannot please God. "So then they that are in the flesh cannot please God" (Rom. 8:8). Our Lord declared: "Light is come into the world, and men loved darkness rather than light" (John 3:19).

Through the prophet Jeremiah, the Spirit of God declared: "The heart is deceitful above all things, and *desperately wicked*" (Jer. 17:9). The Hebrew is much stronger and could be translated: "incurably wicked." Something has to happen before a person can please God, can do God's will because he wants to do it. He must have a new nature, and that is what happens when he is born again (see II Peter 1:4). Until a person is born again he cannot even feel comfortable in a prayer meeting. Think how out of place he would feel in the presence of God and in the company of the redeemed!

C. Man must be born again because he is a lost and condemned sinner.

> For God so loved the world, that he gave his only begotten Son, that whosoever believeth in him should not perish, but have everlasting life . . . . He that believeth on him is not condemned: but he that believeth not is condemned already . . . . (John 3:16, 18).

Without the new birth, man is perishing. What does this mean? The original word rendered "perish" here is variously translated as follows: "Perish"—33 times; "lose"—28 times; "destroy"—23 times; and "be lost"—3 times. As used by our Lord, the word "perish" or "lost" means that in his natural, sinful state, man is eternally lost to the wonderful purpose for which God intended man; namely, to glorify God and enjoy His presence forever. God in His love sent the Son to deliver man from his lost or perishing state and restore him to the purpose of God. Without the new birth, received when a person receives Christ as his own Saviour and Lord, man's situation is absolutely hopeless. To make this very clear, our Lord stated that man is "condemned already." CONDEMNED ALREADY, that is the judicial position of every person without Christ. The position of every person who is "in Christ Jesus" is "Not condemned." This child of God shall not come into condemnation (cf. Rom. 8:1), and "shall never perish" (John 10:28).

While endeavoring to explain the meaning of the new birth, I have often pointed out that everything we will ever have as a result of God's salvation is included in that birth. The same is true in the physical realm of the natural birth. Everything is part of that birth, although many things are not yet evident. There are no teeth, no ability to kick a football or drive a car. But all that is included in that birth—from the teeth to the muscles, even the ability to have children of your own in due time—will become experience. The same is true of the new birth. From justification to resurrection, to glorification (when we shall be like Christ), and everything in between—all are part of our new birth. Of course, some things are not yet apparent, they await the proper time, but the Spirit of God can already say: ". . . [God] hath quickened us together with Christ, ... And hath raised us up together, and *made us sit together in heavenly places* in Christ Jesus" (Eph. 2:5-6).

III. The Holy Spirit's Part in the New Birth

"Wherefore I give you to understand, that no man speaking by the Spirit of God calleth Jesus accursed: and that no man can say that Jesus is the Lord, *but by the Holy Ghost*" (I Cor. 12:3).

From the study of the Word of God we understand that the Holy Spirit has taken over completely the application and the communication of the entire salvation of God which was provided through the Son. Whatever, therefore, the work of the triune God in behalf of man may be during this present age, it is made available to us through the Holy Spirit. In harmony with this truth, I believe that although man is commanded to repent and believe in Christ as Saviour, man would be helpless to do so without the operation of the

Spirit. Without the Spirit's work within man to enlighten and to convict, man would never come to accept Christ as a personal Saviour. This fact is in view in the previous Scripture which declares "that no man can say that Jesus is the Lord, but by the Holy Ghost."

Of course, any man can pronounce the words that declare Jesus as the Lord. Many who were not born again have done just that. But to acknowledge in truth and from the heart Christ as one's own Saviour and Lord, can only come through the enlightenment and conviction of the Holy Spirit. It is reported that one of David Livingstone's first converts in Africa was a tribal chief whose name was Sechele. This chief suggested to Livingstone: "I shall call my headman, and with our whips of rhinoceros-hide we will soon make them all believe together." But whips or anything of the flesh can never make a man believe from the heart, only the Holy Spirit can produce the faith that saves, through the Word of God.

Because of man's helplessness, and since the application of God's salvation for man has been committed to the Holy Spirit, the subject of the Spirit's part in the new birth is certainly a very large one. Most assuredly the Holy Spirit is active in all that pertains to the new birth—from the very start to the very finish. The following is but a partial list of what the Spirit does for every believer at the moment of the new birth:

A. The Spirit imparts new life. "That which is born of the Spirit is spirit . . . . so is every one that is born of the Spirit" (John 3:6, 8). This new life, which the Spirit imparts, is the "eternal life" which Christ has and which He promised to give to those who believe in Him (see John 10:28; I John 5:11-13).

B. The Holy Spirit comes to indwell the believer. "But ye are not in the flesh, but in the Spirit, if so be that the Spirit of God dwell in you. Now if any man have not the Spirit of Christ, he is none of his" (Rom. 8:9). "Know ye not that ye are the temple of God, and that the Spirit of God dwelleth in you?" (I Cor. 3:16).

C. The believer is sealed with the Holy Spirit. This signifies ownership and safe-keeping. "In whom [in Christ] ye also trusted, after that ye heard the word of truth, the gospel of your salvation: in whom also after that ye believed, ye were sealed with that holy Spirit of promise" (Eph. 1:13).

D. The believer is baptized with (or in) the Spirit and is placed in vital union with Christ. "For by one Spirit are we all baptized into one body, whether we be Jews or Gentiles, whether we be bond or free; and have been all made to drink into one Spirit" (I Cor. 12:13). This Spirit baptism will be considered at length in a later chapter.

E. The Holy Spirit becomes the believer's unlimited resource for a successful Christian life.

> O wretched man that I am! who shall deliver me from the body of this death? I thank God through Jesus Christ our Lord .... For the law of the *Spirit of life* in Christ Jesus hath made me free from the law of sin and death (Rom. 7:24-25; 8:2).

Here is a marvelous and meaningful fact: In the seventh chapter of Romans, where the wrong way of trying to live a successful Christian life is described, the Holy Spirit is not once mentioned. In the eighth chapter, where we learn of "the glorious liberty of the children of God" (Rom. 8:21), the Holy Spirit is the center of it all, appearing by name at least 19 times. This fact alone says better than I could say it, that the presence of the Holy Spirit within the believer is the true answer to the quest of a Christian life that will glorify the Lord and be a blessing to others.

The Holy Spirit is present within every born-again person. He wants to fill us with the joy and victory of Christ. He is waiting for us to avail ourselves of His almighty power to enable us to live to the glory of God who redeemed us through Christ. "But the fruit of the Spirit is love, joy, peace, longsuffering, gentleness, goodness, faith, meekness, temperance" (Gal. 5:22-23).

In the early years of my ministry I became acquainted with a family—"Charlie's family." We picked up Charlie's wife and four chidren for Sunday School and church; and after a year all five received the Lord Jesus as their Saviour. You can imagine the prayers that were offered for Charlie. I visited often, hoping to catch Charlie at home and in a good mood. He had a trick for preachers—when one came in the front door he went out the back. One day when I visited the family, he slipped up and had to make a fast dash into the bathroom. Mrs. Charlie and I sat in the living room and talked about the Lord in louder voices than we usually used. In my brief glimpses of Charlie I saw a short, sullen, unhappy man whose bad habits had already marred his young face. The home, the caring wife, the thin children all reflected Charlie's habits. Because of prayer the Holy Spirit was working in Charlie's heart. Even as Paul "kicked against the pricks," Charlie became meaner.

One day at breakfast his five-year-old son said, "Mama, when we go to heaven, daddy won't be there, will he?" What a bombshell! Charlie dashed out of the house to throw away his slim salary in a card game. As he later said, "All I could hear all day were those words ringing in my ears." The Holy Spirit used a few words from an innocent child to do God's work that day. Charlie began to come to church and soon made a decision for the Lord. And it was great to see the transformation that took place. Charlie's face changed first, it was no longer glowering—it glowed! He began to talk freely and testified that God had delivered him from a very bad life. The home got some new furniture, and the children began to fill out a bit from a better diet. We saw visible evidence of a new creation in the Lord. He was a changed man. An experience like this does a lot of good to a preacher and his congregation. This true story is important because it illustrates that the new birth is accomplished through the Holy Spirit. With Charlie, there was much outward evidence of what had happened within his heart. It helped us to understand the relationship of the new birth and the Holy Spirit. In every conversion there is the operation of the Holy Spirit.

Questions for Discussion:

1. What special significance does the word "become" have in John 1:12?

2. How many reasons can you give for the absolute necessity of the new birth?

3. How do you explain the statement found in I Corinthians 12:3: "that no man can say that Jesus is the Lord, but by the Holy Ghost"?

7

I Corinthians 12:12-27

The Baptism of the
Holy Spirit (Part I)

I. **The Biblical Background of Spirit Baptism**
   A. All the references to baptism with the Spirit that are in the four Gospels came from the lips of John the Baptist.
   B. Only once did Christ mention the Baptism of the Spirit, as far as the Bible record goes.
   C. The seventh and last mention of the Baptism of the Spirit is found in I Corinthians 12:13

II. **The Significance of the Baptism of the Spirit**
   A. The Baptism of the Spirit is the sovereign act of God by means of the Spirit, whereby the believer is brought from his position in Adam to his new position in Christ.
   B. The context of I Corinthians 12:13 not only supports, but demands this interpretation of Spirit Baptism.
   C. The rest of the New Testament bears witness to the Baptism of the Spirit which places the believer into the Body of Christ.
   D. This Baptism of the Spirit began on the Day of Pentecost.

III. **Important Characteristics of the Baptism of the Spirit**
   A. The universal experience of all true believers
   B. Not perceived through the five senses of the body
   C. The work of the Holy Spirit which is peculiar to this present age
   D. The spiritual reality of which water baptism is the symbol

There is no aspect of the doctrine of the Holy Spirit which has been as misunderstood and as misused as has His baptism. The basis of this misunderstanding lies in the teaching of the last 100 years that this baptism is a second work of grace which the believer may receive at some time after he has been saved. According to this teaching, Spirit Baptism is supposed to convey to the recipient a special power. The claimed results of this power vary with different groups who adhere to the second-work-of-grace teaching. With some, it is supposed to bring entire sanctification, or a sinless life. To others it means the ability to speak in unknown tongues. With many it adds up to producing spiritual pride, a feeling of spiritual superiority, of being super-Christians. This teaching of the Baptism of the Holy Spirit as a second work of grace is the main basis of Pentecostalism and of the Charismatic movement.

It is doubtless true that many earnest and faithful believers hold to the teaching of the Baptism of the Spirit as a second work of grace. They are sincere in their belief and in their claim of having received such a second work or blessing. This fact makes it difficult to speak out against the teaching. In many instances it is simply a misunderstanding of terms in which the "infilling" of the Spirit is called the "Baptism" of the Spirit.

In a previous chapter, mention has been made of the fact that a great deal of misunderstanding would be avoided if we made a clear distinction between that which the Scriptures command or exhort us to do, and that which God has promised to do for us. That which God asks of us, is our responsibility. That which God promised to do, is His responsibility, and He will surely do it. This distinction is especially important in respect to the infilling and the Baptism of the Spirit. Believers are strongly exhorted to be filled with the Spirit (Eph. 5:18). This infilling depends on the believer. But *never* are believers exhorted to be baptized with or by the Spirit, or to seek such an experience. This baptism is a miracle of God's grace, it is God's gift to every believer, for "by one Spirit *are we all baptized into one body*" (I Cor. 12:13).

While considering the Baptism of the Spirit, we need to remember that sound doctrine must always be based upon what the Word of God says, not upon human experiences or upon the teaching or tradition of a denomination. A thorough study of this baptism may sometimes bring us face to face with the deeper things of the Word. I have learned that in the deep sections of God's Word, some of the most precious truths are hidden. A simple faith in God's Word is the best way to understand the deeper things. And lest anyone might be inclined to be turned off by the prospect of facing deep things, let me tell the following true story on myself:

During the years of World War II, I served as pastor of a congregation in Washington, D.C. The janitor of the church was a rather simple soul who had a deep loyalty toward me. In the front of the church was a lighted bulletin board and it was my practice to announce my Sunday messages on that board. This practice always seemed to fascinate the janitor. One year our choir was presenting an Easter cantata on Sunday evening. So I simply put the letters that spelled CAN-TATA in the line for the evening service. Having finished the job, I returned to my study. Several parishioners observed the janitor as he carefully considered the subjects. When he came to the evening part, he spelled it out syllable by syllable, "CAN-TA-TA." Having spelled it out slowly, he turned to the bystanders and announced solemnly: "I tell you, that man is deep. He is d-e-e-p!" I am afraid that was the only time I was ever considered to be "deep."

Nevertheless the fact remains that there are "the deep things of God" in His Word (I Cor. 2:10). These deep things of God call for careful study on our part, under the guidance of the Holy Spirit of God. Knowledge of the deep things of God is not limited to the intellectual or highly educated person. Jesus said that God has hidden some things from the wise and prudent and has revealed them to babes. A simple, childlike faith is the most important factor in understanding the deep things of God's Word.

I. The Biblical Background of Spirit Baptism

A. All the references to baptism with the Spirit that are in the four Gospels came from the lips of John the Baptist. There are four such references, as follows: Matthew 3:11; Mark 1:8; Luke 3:16; and John 1:33. Since the first three are reports of the same incident, we need to consider only one of them. Matthew quotes John the Baptist as declaring: "I indeed baptize you with water unto repentance: but he that cometh after me is mightier than I, whose shoes I am not worthy to bear: he shall baptize you with the Holy Ghost and with fire" (Matt. 3:11). The Apostle John recorded that the Baptist bore public witness to Jesus as being the Son of God by announcing: "Behold the Lamb of God, which taketh away the sin of the world" (John 1:29). The Baptist climaxed his witness by declaring:

> And I knew him not: but he that sent me to baptize with water, the same said unto me, Upon whom thou shalt see the Spirit descending, and remaining on him, the same is he which baptizeth with the Holy Ghost. And I saw, and bare record that this is the Son of God (vv. 33-34).

Taking all four references in the Gospels together, we gather the following facts: (1) John the Baptist declared that taking away the sin of the world and baptizing with the Holy Spirit would be the great work of Christ. (2) John the Baptist received this information from God (see John 1:33). (3) We learn that Christ is the one who does the baptizing with the Spirit. (4) In each instance this baptizing with the Spirit is said to be at a future time.

B. Only once did Christ mention the Baptism of the Spirit, as far as the Bible record goes. This was after His resurrection, on the day of His ascension. In the first chapter of Acts we read:

And, being assembled together with them, commanded them that they should not depart from Jerusalem, but wait for the promise of the Father, which, saith he, ye have heard of me. For John truly baptized with water; but ye shall be baptized with the Holy Ghost not many days hence (Acts 1:4-5).

Concerning this statement I suggest these observations: (1) Jesus is speaking of the same baptism of which John the Baptist spoke. (2) This baptism was the promise of the Father of which Jesus had told His disciples before (see Acts 1:4, cf. John 14:16-17). (3) This Baptism with the Spirit was still future on the day of Christ's ascension, but only a few days away—"not many days hence." (4) The disciples were to wait in Jerusalem until this baptism occurred. This they did, and 10 days later, the Holy Spirit came.

Whatever this baptism of the Spirit is, it first began on the Day of Pentecost. Peter attested this fact when he defended his action of having baptized and received as a Christian brother, a Gentile, Cornelius by name. Said Peter:

And as I began to speak, the Holy Ghost fell on them, as on us at the beginning. Then remembered I the word of the Lord, how that he said, John indeed baptized with water; but ye shall be baptized with the Holy Ghost. Forasmuch then as God gave them the like gift as he did unto us, who believed on the Lord Jesus Christ; what was I, that I could withstand God? (Acts 11:15-17, cf. Acts 10:44-48).

In this instance we find that Peter declared: (1) that this was the same baptism as they had received; (2) that this baptism was the gift of God; (3) that this gift of God was the gift of the Holy Spirit (cf. Acts 10:44-47).

C. The seventh and last mention of the Baptism of the Spirit by name is found in I Corinthians 12:13: "For by one Spirit are we all baptized into one body, whether we be Jews or Gentiles, whether we be bond or free; and have been all made to drink into one Spirit." This statement is important, for while the prophecy of John the Baptist provided the promise of this baptism, here the spiritual significance is presented. This significance is endorsed and enlarged upon in some of the other Epistles as we shall see a bit later.

Before we deal further with the significance, a word of explanation is needed concerning the change of a preposition. In the other six references to Spirit Baptism, the preposition "with" is used in our translation. The promise was: "Ye shall be baptized *with* the Holy Ghost" (Acts 1:5). Here in the Corinthian passage (12:13) we read: "For *by* one Spirit are we all baptized into one body." The *with* is changed to *by*. In the Greek text there is no such change, the same Greek preposition (en) is used in all seven references to Spirit Baptism. Why the change in our translation? In all the promises by John the Baptist, Christ is said to be the baptizer with the Spirit. The change from *with* to *by* seems to make the Spirit do the baptizing. The question is this: Can the Greek preposition (en) be translated *by* as well as *with*?

According to Greek scholars, the Greek (en) can be translated properly by the preposition *by* when it speaks of the instrument through which something is done, in the sense of doing something "by means of." This is called the "instrumental" use of (en). The New Testament presents many such usages. One of the most vivid examples is found in the accusation of the Pharisees who suggested that Christ "doth not cast out devils, but *by* [en] Beelzebub the prince of the devils" (Matt. 12:24). The accusation was that Christ drove out devils by means of Satan's power.

The Holy Spirit was sent by Christ from the Father (John 15:26, cf. 16:7). He came to apply the salvation which Christ had provided. This work was begun on the Day of Pentecost. From that day on until the Spirit will be removed, *the work of Christ* in and through man on earth is done (en) *by the means of the Holy Spirit.* This work includes the baptism of believers into the Body of Christ.

In the light of the above, we can accept the translation "For *by* one Spirit are we all baptized into one body" as the correct one, if we understand it to mean: "By the means of the Spirit." It is correct because Christ saves, dwells within, keeps, finishes the work which He has begun in us—all by means of the Holy Spirit.

II. The Significance of the Baptism of the Spirit

A. The Baptism of the Spirit is the sovereign act of God by means of the Spirit, whereby the believer is brought from his position in Adam to his new position in Christ. When a person receives Christ as Saviour, he is born again of the Spirit and is placed, immersed into Christ, and thus becomes a member of the Body of Christ. This is henceforth the believer's position. He is in union with Christ and is part of Christ. He is completely identified with Christ—in His death, in His resurrection, and in His future glory.

This union with Christ is the most glorious truth revealed in the New Testament. It is the only basis of our acceptance with God. It is unique for this present age of grace. This union was first made known by our Lord on the night before His crucifixion (as were many of the truths that became reality after His death and resurrection). On that night Jesus declared according to John 14:20: "At that day [the day when the Holy Spirit would be sent, see vv. 16-17] ye shall know that I am in my Father, and *ye in me,* and I in you." "Ye in me," that is the believer's position. In the remainder of His discourse that night, Jesus revealed what this means. As you read chapters 14 through 17 of John's Gospel where that discourse is recorded, you find that being in Christ means that Christ's Father is our Father, His home is our home, His life is our life, His joy is our joy, His peace is our peace, and His resources are our resources. In Christ—this is the believer's position. We are placed there by the operation of the Holy Spirit. This is the spiritual significance of the Baptism of the Spirit.

B. The context of I Corinthians 12:13 not only supports, but demands this interpretation of Spirit Baptism: "For by one Spirit are we all baptized into one body." What body is that? "For as the body is one, and hath many members, and all the members of that one body, being many, are one body, *so also is Christ*" (v. 12). "Now ye are *the body of Christ,* and members in particular" (v. 27). The "body" into which believers are baptized is the Body of Christ, of which He is the head, made up of all true believers. This Body of Christ is the true church (Eph. 1:22-23). The subject of the entire twelfth chapter of I Corinthians is a passionate plea for unity among believers, based upon their being, in fact, members of the one Body of Christ, being placed there by the one Holy Spirit of God.

C. The rest of the New Testament bears witness to the Baptism of the Spirit which places the believer into the Body of Christ. "Know ye not, that so many of us as were baptized into Jesus Christ were baptized into his death?" (Rom. 6:3). This must be Spirit Baptism, for no one but the Holy Spirit can baptize us "into Jesus Christ."

"For as many of you as have been baptized into Christ have put on Christ" (Gal. 3:27). The context of this verse shows that it must also refer to the Baptism of the Spirit. "For ye are all the children of God by faith in Christ Jesus" (v. 26). These children, by faith in Christ, have been "baptized into Christ" (v. 27), and as a result "ye are all one in Christ Jesus" (v. 28). It is my firm belief that the "one baptism" mentioned in Ephesians 4:5 also speaks of the Baptism of the Spirit, as does Colossians 2:12, which reads: "Buried with him in baptism, wherein also ye are risen with him through the faith of the operation of God, who hath raised him from the dead."

D. This Baptism of the Spirit began on the Day of Pentecost (Acts 1:4-5; 11:15-17). Until the Spirit came on Pentecost, this baptism was but a promise for the future. *The reason is that Christ had first to give His life as an atonement for sin before man could be placed in union with Him.* Since this placing into union with Christ was to be the special work of the Spirit during this age, it awaited the Spirit's coming.

Once He had taken up His abode in the members who now formed the Body of Christ, every new believer is baptized into that Body when he receives Christ as Saviour.

III. Important Characteristics of the Baptism of the Spirit

A. This baptism is the universal experience of all true believers. "For by one Spirit *are we all* baptized into one body" (I Cor. 12:13). This is true because it is the gift of God and a part of His salvation by grace. This baptism does not therefore depend upon the believer's degree of spirituality, for it is a positional baptism, that places us in Christ.

B. Like the new birth, the Baptism of the Spirit is not perceived through the five senses of the body. The same thing is true of the sealing of the Spirit. Though very real, the believer may not be conscious of it. This does not mean that the results of the baptism won't bring conscious experiences. Being placed in the Body of Christ is an action of the Holy Spirit which in itself is not felt through the five senses of the body. The following quote from Dr. Walvoord's book *The Holy Spirit* puts the matter very well:

> While our position in Christ is the ground of our experience when we are yielded to the Spirit, our position in itself does not produce experience. All Christians have the same position in Christ, but many have little spiritual experience. While experience may vary and be far from static in any individual, the position of the believer in Christ remains unalterably the same. It is peculiarly evident that the original act of the Spirit, placing us in Christ, produced no sensation.

C. The Baptism of the Spirit is the work of the Holy Spirit which is peculiar to this present age. Through this baptism into Christ, the true Church (which is the Body of Christ) is formed. With this baptism this present age began at Pentecost. When the Church will be completed, Christ will return for her, and the Holy Spirit will be removed with the Church.

D. The Baptism of the Spirit is the spiritual reality of which water baptism is the symbol. Water baptism is the visible symbol of that invisible Baptism of the Spirit. Through the Baptism of the Spirit the believer is placed in union with Christ, is identified with Christ in His death and in His resurrection. "Buried with him in baptism, wherein also ye are risen with him through the faith of the operation of God, who hath raised him from the dead" (Col. 2:12, cf. Rom. 6:3-5). Of this wonderful action of God by means of the Spirit, the baptism in water is the symbol, the visible demonstration. It follows, therefore, that water baptism is for believers, for those who have been baptized by the Spirit. This baptism in water is a command of Christ which has not been recalled. It is also important that when a believer is so baptized in water, he should understand what this action symbolizes. Only then is water baptism a blessing and a testimony.

Questions for Discussion:

1. Which of the following are the believer's responsibility, and which are the sovereign gifts of God?

Repentance	The Baptism of the Spirit
Faith	The Sealing of the Spirit
The New Birth	Water Baptism
Justification	Walking in the Spirit

2. When, and by whom was the believer's union with Christ first mentioned?

3. Where do we find scriptural proof that all believers have received the Baptism of the Spirit?

8

John 17:1-26

The Baptism of the Holy Spirit (Part II)

I. **The Gift of the Holy Spirit Cannot Be a Second Blessing Experienced by Some but Not by All Believers**
   A. A person who does not have the Holy Spirit is not saved.
   B. All believers have the Holy Spirit dwelling within them.

II. **The Baptism of the Holy Spirit Is NOT a Second Blessing**
   A. The Baptism of the Spirit is received by all true believers.
   B. There is no injunction to seek the Baptism of the Holy Spirit.

III. **The Baptism of the Spirit and the Infilling of the Spirit**
   A. The Baptism of the Spirit places the believer into the Body of Christ, and into Christ Himself.
   B. The Baptism of the Spirit is God's sovereign and unconditional work, accomplished in every believer, through, or by means of the Holy Spirit.
   C. The Baptism of the Spirit is a once-for-all experience.

Apparently the greatest concern of our Lord on the last night of His earthly life was the spiritual unity and love among all who would believe on Him. One cannot read His prayer that night, as recorded in chapter 17 of John, without being impressed with this concern. The reason for this great concern was the necessity of spiritual unity and love as a backdrop for the effectiveness of the Gospel. Without this unity, the world would not be persuaded of the reality of Christ as the Saviour of man. The end of the Lord's cry for this unity was: ". . . that the world may believe that thou hast sent me" (John 17:21), ". . . that the world may know that thou hast sent me, and hast loved them, as thou hast loved me" (John 17:23).

The Word of God presents two basic truths side by side. One is the fact that the salvation of man from sin through Jesus Christ is the central passion and purpose of the God who is love. The other truth is that the greatest endeavor of Satan is concentrated on trying to defeat this great purpose of God by keeping as many people as possible from believing in Christ. The Word of God tells us that Satan blinds the minds of the unbelieving: "Lest the light of the glorious gospel of Christ, who is the image of God, should shine unto them" (II Cor. 4:4).

Since the spiritual unity of believers is so very important to the successful presentation of Christ in the world, we are not surprised to find that Satan has worked every angle possible to divide God's people. This is one of the methods by which he weakens the influence of the Gospel. First he causes division (he does not care by what means it is accomplished). Then he plays the division up out of its true proportion, to turn people off, to discredit the Gospel. Thus he tries to blind the minds of the unbelieving to the reality of Christ. This has been going on from the very beginning of the church, as is so vividly demonstrated in Paul's letters to the Corinthians.

It is quite clear that there has to be a clear-cut division

between the true Gospel of Christ and that which is a false or counterfeit gospel. There can be no spiritual union between those who base their salvation upon the atoning death and bodily resurrection of the second person of the Godhead, and those who believe and teach that Christ was no more than a great teacher and reformer. Neither can there be union, or dare there be compromise, between a salvation that is wholly based upon the finished work of Christ, and a salvation that is partly of Christ and partly of man's good works. Paul graphically stated the case to the Galatians among whom this compromise had been introduced.

> I marvel that ye are so soon removed from him that called you into the grace of Christ unto another gospel: which is not another; but there be some that trouble you, and would pervert the gospel of Christ. But though we, or an angel from heaven, preach any other gospel unto you than that which we have preached unto you, let him be accursed (Gal. 1:6-8).

But what about the divisions that exist among Evangelicals? What about the differences between so-called Holiness groups who believe in the Baptism of the Spirit as a second work of grace, and those who insist that the Holy Spirit is received by all believers at the moment of their salvation? Can there be peace and spiritual union between them? What about Pentecostalism with its phenomenal growth and its emphasis on speaking in unknown tongues? Can there be spiritual union between them and those who believe that the gift of tongues ceased when its purpose was fulfilled? And what about the great Charismatic movement that is now sweeping through many churches—is it of God? These are legitimate questions because the Lord prayed earnestly for spiritual unity among believers. These are also important questions, because these bodies and movements are strong and active, and they are not going away.

Since the gift of tongues will be treated later in this book, this present study will deal mainly with the teaching of the Second Blessing. However, it is important that we recognize

the common background of the teaching of the Second Blessing, the Pentecostal movement, and the Charismatic movement. All three movements arose out of a sincere desire to
seek God's best for the Christian life. Believers were dissatis-
fied with the lack of power in their churches and in their own
lives. They wanted to enter experimentally into the power
that God had promised His children. Out of this desire first
came the Holiness movement, which thrived on the teaching
that every believer can have a second spiritual experience in
which he receives the power needed for a victorious life.
Unfortunately, this experience was soon believed to be the
Baptism with the Holy Spirit. Soon it was taught that this
Baptism was to be earnestly sought and could be experienced
at any time after salvation, even years later. Later it took on
the meaning that this experience would provide the recipient
with the power to live a sinless life. Sometimes the teaching
included the claim that as a result of this experience, the old
nature was eradicated so that a person who had the experience of this Second Blessing could not sin.

Out of this Holiness movement grew what became known
as Pentecostalism which grew rapidly, beginning at about the
turn of this century. This movement went a step further in
emphasizing that the Baptism of the Spirit subsequent to
salvation is confirmed by the speaking in an unknown
tongue. Pentecostals believe that what happened on the Day
of Pentecost can, and should, happen today.

The Holiness movement not only was born out of a long-
ing for the power of God; its claims have a strong appeal to
believers everywhere. Who is there among us that is satisfied
with his or her spiritual state? I am not! Yes, I am satisfied
with my position in Christ Jesus and thank God daily that He
has accepted me in "the Beloved," but I am also daily aware
of my lack of spiritual perfection. Now, if there is some
sudden, God-given experience which would once for all set
me free from my unspiritual self, I would not want to miss it.
So the question really is this: Is there such a second, crisis

experience which God has provided, and if so, what is it called in the Word of God?

In trying honestly to find the answer to this question, we must have a touchstone of truth. This touchstone is the Word of God and it alone. We dare not draw our conclusions from human experiences except as they give a living testimony to what the Word teaches. God's Word is "profitable for doctrine, for reproof, for correction, for instruction in righteousness: That the man of God may be perfect, throughly furnished unto all good works" (II Tim. 3:16-17). From the Word, therefore, we must draw our conclusions. Not from man's system of theology. Not from the official or unofficial position of a church or denomination.

In our endeavor to reach the right conclusion, we must consider all that the Word has to say on the subject. We dare not seek to prove our preconceived idea or theory by searching for some Scripture that will support it. This foolish method has given birth to many dangerous heresies. The late Dr. Alva J. McClain used to demonstrate the foolishness of that method by saying: "If you want to be known as a good shot, you first shoot a hole in the barn door. Then you walk up and draw a small circle with the bullet hole right in the center of that circle." Some try to do just that with the Bible. They first believe what they want to believe and find Scripture to prove it. I remember one man who stated his false belief rather emphatically in a prayer meeting. When I asked him to turn to the Scripture which revealed the fallacy of his belief, he read it and then said: "Well, if Paul said that, that part is not inspired." First draw a circle, and then test your marksmanship by seeing how close your shot comes to the center of that circle. That is the proved method of sharpshooting. First find out what God's Word teaches, then shape your belief to fit it. That is the only way to come to the right conclusion in spiritual matters.

With this rather lengthy introduction, let us examine the teaching of a second work of grace in relation to the Holy Spirit.

I. The Gift of the Holy Spirit Cannot Be a Second Blessing Experienced by Some but Not by All Believers

The gift of the Holy Spirit is God's sovereign gift *to every believer.* This is the plain, repeated, emphatic teaching of the Word of God.

A. A person who does not have the Holy Spirit is not saved. "So then they that are in the flesh cannot please God. But ye are not in the flesh, but in the Spirit, if so be that the Spirit of God dwell in you. *Now if any man have not the Spirit of Christ, he is none of his"* (Rom. 8:8-9). The plain sense of this Scripture is that anyone who does not have the Holy Spirit dwelling within, is not saved. It has to follow, therefore, that the Holy Spirit is received the moment a person is saved. Either that, or a person is not really saved when he believes but enters a sort of twilight zone until he receives the Holy Spirit at a later time. But there is no such twilight existence to be found in the Word of God. This Scripture simply leaves no room for the claim that a person may be born again and later on receive the Holy Spirit as a second blessing.

B. All believers have the Holy Spirit dwelling within them. This is the positive side of the question. The Scriptures which declare this are many. The following are among the most prominent:

"Now we have received, not the spirit of the world, but the spirit which is of God" (I Cor. 2:12).

"What? know ye not that your body is the temple of *the Holy Ghost which is in you,* which ye have of God, and ye are not your own? (I Cor. 6:19). Now who are the "ye" in this Scripture who have received the Holy Spirit from God? "Unto the church of God which is at Corinth, to them that are sanctified in Christ Jesus, called to be saints, with all that in every place call upon the name of Jesus Christ our Lord, both their's and our's" (I Cor. 1:2).

The church at Corinth had some spiritual people in it, and also some very carnal believers. Paul called them carnal, and "babes in Christ" (I Cor. 3:1). A carnal Christian is a believer who is still dominated by the flesh. A spiritual Christian is a believer who is yielded to the control of the Holy Spirit of God. A "babe in Christ" is a believer who has not grown up spiritually, either because he has recently been born again, or else he has not developed, has not matured, and still acts like a spiritual baby. Still, the apostle, who was led by the Spirit to write these words, insisted that all those who believed, both in Corinth and everywhere else, have received the Holy Spirit from God and are indwelt by that Spirit.

"And because ye are sons, God hath sent forth the Spirit of his Son into your hearts, crying, Abba, Father" (Gal. 4:6).

"And he that keepeth his commandments dwelleth in him, and he in him. And hereby we know that he abideth in us, *by the Spirit which he hath given us*" (I John 3:24).

"Hereby know we that we dwell in him, and he in us, because *he hath given us of his Spirit*" (I John 4:13).

A very enlightening passage is found in the short Epistle of Jude. The inspired writer had been warning about false teachers who denied "the only Lord God, and our Lord Jesus Christ" (v. 4). In verse 19 he describes them: "These be they who separate themselves, sensual, *having not the Spirit.*" The same Greek word that is translated "sensual" here is translated "natural" in I Corinthians 2:14: "But the natural man receiveth not the things of the Spirit of God: for they are foolishness unto him: neither can he know them, because they are spiritually discerned." The "natural man" is an unsaved person, and unsaved people are described as "having not the Spirit" (Jude 19).

Letting the Word of God speak, we simply have to come to the conclusion that *all believers have received the gift of the Holy Spirit and are indwelt by Him.* This gift therefore cannot be a second blessing which depends upon believers meeting certain conditions.

II. The Baptism of the Holy Spirit Is NOT a Second Blessing

The meaning of the Baptism of the Holy Spirit has been treated at some length in the preceding chapter. I suggest that the student go over those pages once again with the open Bible before him.

A. The Baptism of the Spirit is received by all true believers. "For *by one Spirit are we all baptized* into one body, whether we be Jews or Gentiles, whether we be bond or free; and have been all made to drink into one Spirit" (I Cor. 12:13). The words "we all" certainly exclude the possibility of this baptism being the experience of some believers and not of others. Again I call attention to the fact that among the "we all" were some who were carnal, not really controlled by the Spirit. But if they were born again, they were part of the Body of Christ, for by means of the Spirit they had been placed there. Weak members, but members nevertheless. "Babes," when they should have been mature—but members of Christ.

B. There is no injunction to seek the Baptism of the Holy Spirit. Not a single command is given to be baptized with the Spirit. No instruction is found on how to be baptized with the Spirit. Not once are believers exhorted to be baptized by the Holy Spirit. This is so because it is the sovereign work of God through the Holy Spirit, bestowed unconditionally upon every person who receives Christ as Saviour and Lord. We can only conclude, therefore, that we should not pray for what we already have received, but should believe God's Word in the matter and act upon the fact. For a born-again person to pray for the Baptism of the Spirit is just as unscriptural as for him to pray for eternal life. Of course, some believers do that, too!

III. The Baptism of the Spirit and the Infilling of the Spirit

There really is a second (third, fourth, fifth?) blessing available to every believer. This blessing is to be *filled* with the Holy Spirit. This filling of the Spirit is by far the most important aspect of all the Spirit's ministry to the believer.

Much of the confusion that has arisen concerning the Baptism of the Spirit as a Second Blessing is due to a misuse of Biblical terminology. Some well-meaning believers who have experienced a real blessing mistakenly call being filled with the Spirit the "Baptism of," or "with the Spirit." However, the two terms are very different. Because of its importance for the believer, a special chapter will be devoted to the study of the Filling of the Spirit later in this book. For the present, I am calling attention to the differences between the Infilling and the Baptism.

A. The Baptism of the Spirit places the believer into the Body of Christ, and into Christ Himself (I Cor. 12.12-13; Rom. 6:3-4). This establishes the believer's position in Christ. This position is the basis of all the believer's spiritual blessings both now and for all eternity.

The filling of the Spirit has to do with the Holy Spirit being in control of the believer's life, enabling the believer to live and serve as God would have him live and serve. The filling is for power—His power.

B. The Baptism of the Spirit is God's sovereign and unconditional work, accomplished in every believer, through, or by means of the Holy Spirit. The believer is never asked or exhorted to seek it or to pray for it.

The filling is the Holy Spirit's response to the believer's yielding to the Spirit's control, so that He takes over, giving the believer the power to live for the glory of God. *Believers* are exhorted *to be filled* with the Spirit. This is God's will for them. It is, therefore, the believer's responsibility to yield to the control of, and to completely rely upon the Holy Spirit of God for spiritual power. "Wherefore be ye not unwise, but understanding what the will of the Lord is. And be not drunk with wine, wherein is excess; *but be filled with the Spirit*" (Eph. 5:17-18).

C. The Baptism of the Spirit is a once-for-all experience. It is never repeated. There is only "one baptism" (Eph. 4:4-5).

The filling with the Spirit may be repeated many times. It

may be lost and renewed. The believer is indwelt by the Holy Spirit, but the Spirit may be grieved by sin and disobedience. He may also be quenched and resisted, and thus He cannot fill the believer as He desires. He does not take over in our lives unless we really want Him to.

We read of repeated filling with the Spirit of the same people in the Book of Acts. "And *they were all filled* with the Holy Ghost, and began to speak with other tongues, as the Spirit gave them utterance" (Acts 2:4). "And when they had prayed, the place was shaken where they were assembled together; and *they were all filled with the Holy Ghost,* and they spake the word of God with boldness" (Acts 4:31).

The Spirit of God filled the apostles and enabled them to do what they could never have done in the flesh. As a new crisis arose, there was prayer, trusting, and a new filling that enabled them to meet each crisis. This is the experience of many believers who have come to see their inability to live Christian lives in their own strength and who surrender fully to the Holy Spirit. A wonderful spiritual experience follows and their lives are filled with joy and victory. In the Word of God this is called "being filled with the Holy Ghost." But because of tradition or teaching, many are calling the experience the Baptism of, (or being baptized with) the Holy Spirit.

Someone may want to ask: "Does it really matter what we call it, as long as we have the experience?" Yes, it does matter very much. A great deal of confusion, misunderstanding, and even mistrust among believers are present due to the use of the wrong term for the filling of the Spirit. This situation has aided Satan in his endeavor to divide God's people. Believers are exhorted to "all speak the same thing" (I Cor. 1:10). A very strong responsibility rests upon all who teach and preach the Word of God to be diligent and careful in "rightly dividing the word of truth" (II Tim. 2:15).

I happen to believe that strong and constant teaching of the whole Word of God is the answer to all the ills that try to invade the Body of Christ, the Church. When believers are well taught in all the truth, they will know the way out of spiritual defeat and failure to victory and joy in the Lord. Sound teaching of the Word will fortify them against false teaching which Satan tries to sneak in. Sound and enthusiastic teaching of the Word will lead to witnessing and to a strong interest in missions. Sound Bible teaching must include the presentation of the person and ministry of the Holy Spirit (the dispenser of all the grace of God) and the believer's response to this ministry. Paul's parting words to the elders of the church at Ephesus are very pertinent here:

> For I have not shunned to declare *unto you all the counsel of God.* Take heed therefore unto yourselves, and to all the flock, over the which the Holy Ghost hath made you overseers, to feed the church of God, which he hath purchased with his own blood (Acts 20:27-28).

The Lord does not want His people to be divided. The devil does want to divide them and uses every opportunity to promote division. Yes, we work together with, and have fellowship with those bodies that hold to a second work of grace and who mistake the "Filling of the Spirit" for the "Baptism of the Spirit." But, how much sweeter would be the fellowship, and how much closer the bond, if the disagreement were not there as a fly in the ointment! May the Holy Spirit of God be our patience and our wisdom in *searching* and *teaching,* and in *believing* God's Word!

Questions for Discussion:

1. What is the difference between a carnal and a spiritual Christian?

2. How many different Scriptures can you turn to that declare that a believer is indwelt by the Holy Spirit?

3. Since spiritual unity among believers is so important to an effective presentation of Christ to the world, how far should we go to present such a united front?

9

Acts 10

Questions That
Must Be Answered

I. Does not the Scripture say: "Have ye received the Holy Ghost since ye believed?"
   A. The context reveals that Paul was talking to non-Christians.
   B. The word "since," as translated in the Authorized Version, is very misleading.

II. Is not obedience one of the scriptural conditions for receiving the Holy Spirit?
   A. The context shows that Peter was speaking to unbelievers.
   B. The "obedience" in view here is the response of faith to the hearing of the Gospel.

III. Acts 8:14-17
   A. The context reveals that Philip, one of the original deacons, went to the city of Samaria and preached Christ to the Samaritans.
   B. But why was there a delay in their receiving of the Holy Spirit?

Have you ever been puzzled by a certain Scripture and decided to consult a commentary? As you found the correct place in the commentary, did you discover that the writer said a great deal about what you already knew, and simply ignored that part of the verse you did not understand? Disgustedly you opened another commentary and were you disappointed again? Well, it has happened to all of us. I would not mind it if the writer simply said: "I don't know what this means," but simply to ignore it—that is not fair.

After having asserted in the last two chapters that the Baptism of the Holy Spirit is the sovereign work of the Holy Spirit whereby He brings us into the Body of Christ, there are some questions that need to be answered. I have tried to demonstrate from the Word of God that the gift of the Holy Spirit is part of the gift of salvation and that He comes to indwell every believer at the moment he is born again. There are many Scriptures that teach this. However, there are passages which are used by those who hold to the belief that the gift of the Holy Spirit is a second work of grace, received subsequent to salvation, and upon meeting certain conditions. Those Scriptures have not been dealt with so far in this Study Guide. This was not an oversight, but I felt they deserved a full chapter.

In any honest and profitable study of the Word of God, certain principles must be observed. When these principles are ignored, the student will become utterly frustrated. One of these principles is that the Bible cannot contradict itself because it is the Word of God. Consequently, when a truth is plainly taught, any statement that seems to contradict that truth must be studied carefully. When this is done, not only is the difficulty removed, but some hitherto missed facet of the truth shines through.

A second principle to remember in the study of God's Word is that different Scriptures belong to different dispensations or ages. The following example will serve to demonstrate this: Jesus sent forth the twelve, and carefully instructed them: *"Go not into the way of the Gentiles, and into any city of the Samaritans enter ye not"* (Matt. 10:5). But Jesus also commanded them: "Ye shall be witnesses unto me both in Jerusalem, and in all Judaea, and *in Samaria*, and unto *the uttermost part of the earth"* (Acts 1:8).

Obviously, the two commands are opposites. But when considered in the light of dispensational truth, the problem is gone and a strong testimony to the trustworthiness of the Scripture remains. The first command was given before the cross, when Christ was still offering the kingdom to Israel with Himself as the king. The second command was after Calvary and just prior to Pentecost when the Spirit would come to usher in the new age. The kingdom belongs to Israel. But during this present age Israel is set aside and the Gospel is offered to all people alike. When this age is completed, Israel will again become God's instrument, will endure great trials, be converted, and finally receive her rightful king and kingdom. The consideration of dispensations is essential in arriving at the right understanding of God's Word. This is included in Paul's admonition: "Study to shew thyself approved unto God, a workman that needeth not to be ashamed, rightly dividing the word of truth" (II Tim. 2:15).

We dare not divorce a statement in God's Word from its immediate context. By this practice most cults find some Scripture to back their false claims.

I. Does not the Scripture say: "Have ye received the Holy Ghost since ye believed?" (Acts 19:2; cf. vv. 1-7).

Yes, this is what it says in our Authorized Version, and this question of Paul has served as the mainstay of teachers of the gift of the Holy Spirit as a second work of grace. But actually this question of the apostle serves as a strong testimony to Paul's often-stated belief that all believers receive the Holy Spirit at the moment of salvation.

A. The context reveals that Paul was talking to non-Christians. In his missionary travels Paul came to Ephesus. There he found certain disciples of John the Baptist. Paul evidently sensed that something was wrong with the object of their faith. So he asked them the leading question, "Have ye received the Holy Ghost since ye believed?" Their response was that they had not even heard of the Spirit. Upon hearing this, Paul asked: "Unto what then were ye baptized?" (Acts 19:3). Their answer explained what was wrong. They had been baptized by John's baptism of repentance.

These men only knew John's message—which was that the Saviour was soon to appear. Some of John's disciples had apparently come to Ephesus. They were still looking for the Christ to come. They had not heard of Calvary, the resurrection, or Pentecost. They must have been thrilled when Paul explained that Christ had come and brought a finished salvation. They readily received Christ and immediately received the Holy Spirit. They were, in fact, filled with the Spirit and spoke with tongues and prophesied. It is interesting to find that when Paul saw their ignorance of the Spirit, he did not instruct them on how to receive *the Spirit.* Rather, he instructed them concerning the person of Christ (19:4). Paul knew that when they received Christ, they would also receive the Holy Spirit as part of God's salvation.

B. The word "since," as translated in the Authorized Version, is very misleading. The Greek text forbids a translation that would have Paul suggesting the receiving of the Holy Spirit sometime after they had become believers. The Greek word is *pisteusantes.* It is an aorist participle which literally means "having believed." The Revised Version translates: "Did you receive the Holy Spirit when you believed?" The Berkeley Version translates: "On you becoming believers?"

The Scofield Reference Bible carries the following significant note on Paul's question:

In both this passage and 1:8 the Greek participles have been translated in such a way that some have concluded that the gift of the Holy Spirit was granted to believers some time after the exercise of faith on their part. The original language allows no such interpretation. The literal translation of 1:8 is "But ye shall receive power, the Holy Spirit coming upon you. . . ." The literal translation of 19:2 is: "He said unto them, Did ye receive the Holy Spirit, having believed?" Both passages could not be stronger in indicating that the Holy Spirit was given at the time of believing (New Scofield Edition, page 1192).

Conclusion: The question of Paul clearly indicates that he expected all true believers to have received the Holy Spirit at the time of believing. To use his question as proof or support of receiving the Holy Spirit some time after salvation, is to ignore the evidence.

II. Is not obedience one of the scriptural conditions for receiving the Holy Spirit?

The Scripture referred to by this question is found in Acts 5:32: "And we are his witnesses of these things; and so is also the Holy Ghost, whom God hath given to them that obey him."

The answer to the above question is very simple. The "obedience" necessary to receiving the Holy Spirit is obedience to the Gospel, the obedience which results in receiving Christ as Saviour. However, this statement by Peter has been used to teach that the coming of the Spirit into the believer's life depends upon the believer living a life of obedience to God. As a matter of fact, *nobody* can possibly live a life of obedience to God except the Holy Spirit dwell within him and enable him to live in obedience.

A. The context shows that Peter was speaking to unbelievers. His words were addressed to the "council," with the High Priest presiding (Acts 5:27-28). Peter, backed by the other apostles, charged the members of the council with the willful murder of Jesus, whom God had raised from the dead (vv. 29-31). Then came the claim that the apostles were witnesses of those things and so was the Holy Spirit "whom God *hath given* to them that obey him" (v. 32). At that the members of the council became furious and would have killed the apostles, had not Gamaliel reasoned them out of it.

B. The "obedience" in view here is the response of faith to the hearing of the Gospel. The apostles had received the Spirit because they had believed in Christ as their Saviour. They had obeyed God in this. Now notice the past tense: "The Holy Ghost, whom God *hath given* to them that obey him." Peter spoke of the obedience of faith in Christ. A short time later some of the Jewish leaders did turn to Christ. Significantly, their conversion is described as follows: "And the word of God increased; and the number of the disciples multiplied in Jerusalem greatly; and a great company of the priests *were obedient to the faith*" (Acts 6:7).

Conclusion: Obedience to the Gospel is necessary to salvation and to the receiving of the Holy Spirit. All who have obeyed the Gospel have been saved and have received the Holy Spirit.

III.

> Now when the apostles which were at Jerusalem heard that Samaria had received the word of God, they sent unto them Peter and John: Who, when they were come down, prayed for them, that they might receive the Holy Ghost: (For as yet he was fallen upon none of them: only they were baptized in the name of the Lord Jesus). Then laid they their hands on them, and they received the Holy Ghost (Acts 8:14-17).

A. The context reveals that Philip, one of the original deacons, went to the city of Samaria and preached Christ to the Samaritans. Many responded and were baptized. When the apostles at Jerusalem heard about it, they sent Peter and John to investigate. They seemed to be satisfied that this was of God and conducted a laying-on-of-hands service, praying that the Holy Spirit would come upon those converts. There was evidence that the Spirit was now received by these people. We are not told the nature of the evidence. But the explanation is plain that until that time they had not received the Spirit (v. 16).

There seems to have been a lapse of time between conversion and the receiving of the Spirit in this case. If there was such a delay, it is the only exception in regard to receiving the Spirit that is reported in the New Testament. To consider their experience as a norm for all believers is as unwarranted as to take Paul's conversion experience as a norm of conversion. His conversion experience certainly was an exception.

B. But why was there a delay in their receiving of the Holy Spirit? If an exception was made, there must have been a good reason for it. To begin with, we observe that the Word does not tell us here why the exception was made. Therefore we have no leave to be dogmatic with our answers. However, searching the New Testament for a reason, I believe we do not have to look very far for the answer.

The last words of our Lord to His disciples were: "But ye shall receive power, after that the Holy Ghost is come upon you: and ye shall be witnesses unto me both in Jerusalem, and in all Judaea, and in Samaria, and unto the uttermost part of the earth" (Acts 1:8). This commission involved three kinds of people: the Jews, the Samaritans, and the Gentiles. Until Philip crossed the threshold, the Gospel had been presented only to the Jews. It was high time that the Samaritans and the Gentiles heard about God's salvation.

(1) Originally, Christ had promised the apostles (and Peter in particular) "the keys of the kingdom of heaven" (Matt. 16:19). Keys are a sign of authority to open closed doors. Did Peter use these keys? He used them on the Day of Pentecost when he opened the door of opportunity for salvation to the Jews (cf. Acts 2:36-41). Later on he opened the door of opportunity to the Gentiles. But that took some doing on God's part, for the Jews never expected God to have anything to do with the Gentiles. To understand the patience of God with Peter in this matter, we need to read chapter 10 of Acts. It is important to observe that the evidence to Peter that God saved Gentiles was that they had received the Holy Spirit. In fact, on that occasion the Holy Spirit was received the moment the people believed, while Peter was still preaching, and before any had been baptized with water

(Acts 10:44-48). When called on the carpet for admitting Gentiles, Peter defended his action by telling the apostles that the evidence of the Gentiles receiving the Holy Spirit had convinced him. As a result of Peter's testimony, the people glorified God and said: "Then hath God also to the Gentiles granted repentance unto life" (Acts 11:18).

All this becomes even more meaningful when we consider Peter's public statement at the first church council in Jerusalem, where the question was resolved whether Gentiles must be circumcised and live like Jews in order to be saved:

> And when there had been much disputing, Peter rose up, and said unto them, Men and brethren, ye know how that a good while ago God made choice among us, *that the Gentiles by my mouth* should hear the word of the gospel, and believe (Acts 15:7).

Then he cited the evidence of God's work among the Gentiles: "And God . . . bare them witness, *giving them the Holy Ghost, even as he did unto us*" (v. 8). He ended his address with this tremendous testimony: "But we believe that through the grace of the Lord Jesus Christ we [believing Jews] shall be saved, even as they [believing Gentiles]" (v. 11). Peter had come a long way from his former position!

Between Pentecost—when Peter offered the Gospel to the Jews—and the time when he opened the door to the Gentiles at the house of Cornelius, there was the experience with the Samaritans. Did Peter open the door there, too?

(2) The Samaritans were a mixed race, descendants of the tribes of Manasseh and Ephraim, and pagan colonists who had been sent to Samaria by the Syrian conqueror. They had their own Scriptures (the first five books of the Old Testament), their own temple at Mt. Gerizim, and claimed to be the only truly orthodox people of God. The Jews despised the Samaritans whom they regarded as a mongrel people. The term "Samaritan" was one of bitter contempt. It was this word that the Jews used to insult Jesus, saying: "Say we not well that thou art a Samaritan, and hast a devil?" (John

8:48). The Apostle John informs us: ". . . for the Jews have no dealings with the Samaritans" (John 4:9).

Now some Samaritans had become Christians. The apostles sent Peter and John to investigate. As they conducted a laying on of hands, the Samaritans received the gift of the Holy Spirit. What the evidence was that they had received the Spirit, we do not know, but Peter and John were convinced; and these people were received as part of the Christian brotherhood.

Conclusion: The following facts stand out: (a) Jesus had given Peter and the apostles "the keys of the kingdom of heaven," representing authority to open doors. (b) Christ had commanded the apostles to witness concerning Him to the Jews, to the Samaritans, and to the Gentiles. (c) God used Peter in each new extension of the Gospel—to the Jews, to the Samaritans, to the Gentiles. (d) In each new extension, the convincing evidence that it was God's doing was the gift of the Holy Spirit.

Knowing that the Jews had "no dealings with the Samaritans," there was evidently great danger that the all-Jewish church would not have recognized the Samaritans as brothers and sisters in Christ. So the civil war which had been carried on between them for centuries would likely have carried over into Christianity. In His sovereign will and wisdom, God withheld the gift of the Holy Spirit from the Samaritans until Peter and John were present as the authorized agents of Christ and as representatives of the apostles. When the Samaritans received the Spirit through the mediacy of Peter and John, all doubts about this being God's work vanished, and the Samaritan converts were received as members of the Body of Christ. As Dr. Ryrie suggests in his book, *The Holy Spirit:* "This delay in the giving of the Spirit saved the early church from having two mother churches—one in Jerusalem and one in Samaria—early in her history. It preserved the unity of the church in this early stage."

While this seems to be the most reasonable explanation of

the delay in the giving of the Spirit at Samaria, we cannot be dogmatic in our presentation. It does fit into the plan of our Lord for the expansion of the Gospel through the agency of the apostles. It also is the interpretation presented by such able Bible teachers as Lewis Sperry Chafer, Charles Caldwell Ryrie, Lehman Strauss, John F. Walvoord, Merrill F. Unger, W. A. Crisswell, J. Dwight Pentecost, David Ewert, Frederick Dale Bruner, Réne Pache, John R. Stott, and others.

Practical Applications:

A. **Behold the amazing grace of God!** The Holy Spirit performed miracles of grace to convince the all-Jewish apostles and the all-Jewish Early Church that God is no respector of persons. He accepts all who will come to Him through faith in Christ, whether Jews, Samaritans, or Gentiles (Rom. 1:16; 10:12-13).

B. **The indwelling Holy Spirit desires to remove all barriers between believers—whether they be social, racial or other barriers, filling our lives with the love of God (Rom. 5:5).** Oh, that we in this twentieth century would be so yielded to Him as were the believers in the first century, when the world looked on in wonder and said: "Behold these Christians, how they love one another!"

As an illustration of this spiritual bond of love that removes all barriers, I cite the following personal experience: It was the first Sunday of 1942, just four weeks after Pearl Harbor. I was pastor of the First Brethren Church in Washington, D.C., in charge of the services. Our guest speaker was a born-again Jew, representing the American Board of Missions to the Jews. As part of the morning worship, we had a baptismal service during which I baptized a young man who was a full-blooded Japanese and in whose conversion I had a little part. America was at war with Germany and with Japan. Here was a unique situation: While hatred was visible everywhere, we had a German for a pastor, a Jew to tell us of Jesus, and a Japanese being welcomed into the fellowship. The Jews were suffering terribly under the Nazi regime in Germany. Americans were being killed and mistreated by Japanese. The F.B.I. investigated me closely (I was glad they were on the job), and they hardly let the Japanese get out of their sight. But in Christ Jesus, we had wonderful fellowship, because the same Holy Spirit indwelt us, shedding abroad in our hearts the very love of God.

Questions for Discussion:

1. What are "dispensations"; and why is it important to know them in teaching the Word of God?

2. What was the baptism of John the Baptist called? (cf. Acts 19:4).

3. What is the important difference between "have ye received the Holy Ghost *since* ye believed?" and "have you received the Holy Spirit *when* you believed?"

4. What is the obedience necessary to the receiving of the Holy Spirit? (cf. Acts 5:32).

10

Romans 8:1-14

The Infilling
of the Holy Spirit

I. **The Meaning or Nature of Being Filled with the Spirit**
   A. Being filled with the Spirit does not mean that we have more of the Spirit.
   B. The filling with the Spirit may be lost and repeated.
   C. Being filled with the Spirit is the believer's responsibility.
   D. The purpose of being filled with the Spirit is to enable the believer to live a spiritually successful life.

II. **The Conditions or Prerequisites of Being Filled with the Spirit**
   A. We must recognize two basic facts: that of our own helplessness, and that we are indwelt by the Holy Spirit.
   B. There must be an earnest desire to be filled.
   C. There must be confession and forsaking of known sin.
   D. Unreserved submission to God

III. **The Results of Being Filled with the Spirit**
   A. The Spirit will make Christ real to the believer.
   B. A Christ-like character will be formed.
   C. The Spirit will give victory over the flesh, the sin-principle.
   D. He will give power for joyful service.

"And be not drunk with wine, wherein is excess; but be filled with the Spirit" (Eph. 5:18).

Dwight L. Moody was a shoe store clerk in Boston when he was led to Christ. We are told that some time after his conversion he heard a great preacher from England say: "The world has yet to see what God can do through a human life that is completely yielded to the Holy Spirit." On hearing that, Mr. Moody is supposed to have said: "By God's grace I want to be that man." We all know something about what God did through that Spirit-filled man whose life meant more to evangelical Christianity in America than the life of any other human being.

As far as the Christian life is concerned, the filling of the Spirit is by far the most important and the most practical aspect of the whole doctrine of the Holy Spirit. To be filled with the Spirit is the greatest need of the believer for a successful, God-honoring, and joyful Christian life. It is therefore with a feeling of awe and of personal inadequacy that I present this study.

I. The Meaning or Nature of Being Filled with the Spirit

To be filled with the Holy Spirit means that a person is controlled by the Holy Spirit. The Spirit imparts to the person spiritual powers and qualities which it is impossible for unaided humanity to have.

The injunction to "be filled with the Spirit" in Ephesians 5:18 is preceded by the injunction: "*Be not* drunk [filled] with wine, wherein is excess." When one is filled with wine, alcohol enters the bloodstream and takes control of the person's faculties. The result is "excess." The Greek word for it is *asotia*—describing a condition in which a person has lost control of himself. Alcohol has taken over and made him a changed person who does silly and foolish things that he would not do otherwise.

"But *be filled* with the Spirit." As the alcohol in the bloodstream takes over and makes a person do unnatural things, so the Holy Spirit—when in control of the Christian—changes him so that his actions and attitudes are in full harmony with the will of God. A number of observations are in order at this point.

A. Being filled with the Spirit does not mean that we have more of the Spirit. However, we will have more of His control and of His power. The Holy Spirit is a person and when He indwells us, we have all of Him. However, the Holy Spirit will only control where He is wanted, and much of the believer's life can be withheld from the Spirit's control. The human personality is a wonderfully complex instrument with such intrinsic components as a will; emotions; attitudes; disposition; temper; the ability to love, to hate, to reason, to speak, to choose, to teach, to plan, to bring joy or sorrow, to be a blessing or a curse, to encourage or to discourage, to pray in the spirit, to witness, to worship, to keep silent. These are but a small fraction of the whole. When the Holy Spirit fills a person, He is in control of the whole person—of all the abilities—and He can really turn a Saul into a Paul, and a cursing Peter into a bold and witnessing apostle.

B. The filling with the Spirit may be lost and repeated. This is not a once-for-all experience. The Greek verb which is translated "be filled" is *plerousthe* and is in the present tense, indicating a continuing experience. Williams translates: "But ever be filled with the Spirit." This meaning is confirmed by the documented experiences of repeated fillings in the Early Church.

In the Book of Acts we read that the first Christians were filled at one time and later were filled again as a new crisis or a new challenge arose for a new enablement from the Holy Spirit. As we compare Acts 2:4 with 4:8 and 4:31, we discover that some of the same persons were filled on several occasions. Paul was first filled when Ananias brought him the message of God in Damascus (Acts 9:17-18). Another special filling is reported in Acts 13:9, at an event that took place a number of years later. The filling of the Spirit may be received, lost, and regained, depending upon the believer.

C. Being filled with the Spirit is the believer's responsibility. "And be not drunk with wine ... but be filled with the Spirit" (Eph. 5:18). Both statements ("be not drunk" and "but be filled") are imperatives in the Greek. This means they are orders, or injunctions, indicating that it is the will of God for every Christian.

The Holy Spirit is present in every believer in all the power of almighty God. He is eager and ready to lead and enable the believer in a joyful, victorious life that will be a blessing to others and pleasing to God. Once more I call attention to the fact that believers are never exhorted or commanded to be baptized with the Holy Spirit. This is so because Spirit-baptism is a positional action of God which establishes our relationship with Christ. The filling with the Spirit is not positional, but has to do with the day-to-day life of the Christian and with his service for his Lord. This is God's enablement which is available to every believer. It is God's declared will that every Christian should take advantage of this gracious provision. It is the believer's responsibility to do so.

D. The purpose of being filled with the Spirit is to enable the believer to live a spiritually successful life. "This I say then, Walk in the Spirit, and ye shall not fulfil the lust of the flesh" (Gal. 5:16).

Once a person has become a child of God through faith in Christ, he has a choice of living by the control of the Holy Spirit, or under the control of the "flesh." If the Holy Spirit is in control, the characteristics of Christ will mark that person's life. If the flesh or self is in control, the characteristics of the flesh will mark that life. A Christian dominated by the flesh is called "carnal" in the Word of God (I Cor. 3:1-3). The word "carnal" means fleshly, or dominated by the desires of the flesh. It is significant to discover that the Corinthian Christians were all baptized with the Spirit (I Cor. 12:13), were second to none in spiritual gifts (1:5-7), but many were carnal (not filled with the Spirit). They were displaying the marks of being dominated by the flesh. Some of those marks were spiritual immaturity, childishness, envy, strife, not being sensitive toward sin, suing each other at the courts of the world, and even getting drunk at the communion service.

Considering such conditions, John R. Stott wrote the following in his excellent booklet entitled, *The Baptism and Fullness of the Holy Spirit:*

> Is not the condition of these Corinthians the state of many of us today? We cannot deny that, according to Scripture, we have been baptized with the Spirit because we have repented and believed, and our water baptism has signified and sealed our Spirit-baptism. But are we filled with the Spirit? That is the question.

II. The Conditions or Prerequisites of Being Filled with the Spirit

A. We must recognize two basic facts: that of our own helplessness, and that we are indwelt by the Holy Spirit. Both facts are so simple, and yet so elusive to us proud humans. The Christian life is a supernatural life. It is just as impossible for a believer to live a successful Christian life in his own strength, as it is for a person to save himself by his own goodness or good works. And yet, almost all of us have had a try at it. It seems that man is addicted to trusting in his own ability to save himself *and* to live a godly life in his own strength. But before the Spirit of God can take over your life and mine, we must come to the end of ourselves and say with Paul (and mean it): "For I know that in me (that is, in my flesh,) dwelleth no good thing: for to will is present with me; but how to perform that which is good I find not" (Rom. 7:18).

Romans 8:1-14 presents an eloquent commentary on the two basic facts that must be recognized before the Spirit can fill our lives. In these verses the apostle is talking about the flesh versus the Spirit of God. He states: "Because the carnal mind is enmity against God . . . . So then they that are in the flesh cannot please God" (vv. 7-8). Jesus insisted that "no man can serve two masters" (Matt. 6:24). Likewise it is impossible to be controlled by the Holy Spirit as long as a person will not "deny self." In other words, the Holy Spirit will not fill us as long as we are filled with ourselves.

We must also recognize that we are indwelt by the Holy Spirit and that He is present within us to provide the enablement needed to live for the glory of God. The Holy Spirit is mentioned 13 times in verses 1-14 of Romans 8. This is God Himself dwelling within us. But, it is one thing to believe this as a doctrine (as something in the Bible)—it is something else to really believe this *as a living reality within us.* Like Martha of old we can be very orthodox and believe the Bible, without it being a living reality to us. When Jesus told Martha that her brother would rise again, her answer was in effect: "O sure, I know about that, he will rise again in the resurrection of the last day." In His patience Jesus said: "I am the resurrection . . . . believest thou this?" (John 11:25-26). Again she said that she believed. But later when Jesus asked to have the stone rolled away from the door of the tomb, Martha protested. She believed, but it was a sort of official impersonal believing—not a vital, living, personal reality. Is the fact that the Holy Spirit dwells within us, a living, vital reality, or just an impersonal, official belief? Just think, God dwells within me! And He is almighty! He is available to me in all His power!

B. There must be an earnest desire to be filled: "If any man *thirst,* let him come unto me, and drink . . . . (But this spake he of the Spirit . . . . " (John 7:37-39). "Blessed are they which do *hunger* and *thirst* after righteousness: for they shall be filled" (Matt. 5:6). "As the hart panteth after the water brooks, so panteth my soul after thee, O God. My soul thirsteth for God, for the living God . . . ." (Ps. 42:1-2).

Hunger and thirst are painful longings or desires. To be filled speaks of having the desire satisfied. To drink will satisfy the thirst. When we come to the place where we are painfully sick of our own failures in the Christian life and want more than anything else to live for God and be a blessing to others, then the way is nearly open for the Holy Spirit to take control.

C. There must be confession and forsaking of known sin. Unconfessed and unforsaken sin causes fellowship with Christ to be broken. Known sin, therefore, makes being filled with the Spirit impossible. Sin must be confessed and forsaken. A confession that is not accompanied by an earnest desire to forsake and be done with the sin, because it grieves God, is not a confession in the spiritual sense.

The two appeals of the inspired apostle: "And grieve not the holy Spirit of God" (Eph. 4:30), and "Be filled with the Spirit" (Eph. 5:18), are surrounded by a list of sins that grieve the Holy Spirit and which prevent Him from filling our lives. The list includes lying, anger, dishonesty, impurity, corrupt speech, bitterness, malice, clamour, evil speaking, fornication, covetousness, filthiness, foolish talking, and jesting. Years later the apostle wrote: "If a man therefore purge himself from these, he shall be a vessel unto honour, sanctified, and meet [fit] for the master's use" (II Tim. 2:21).

D. Unreserved submission to God. This is the most fundamental requirement for the Spirit-filled life.

What, know ye not that your body is the temple of the Holy Ghost which is in you, which ye have of God, and ye are not your own? For ye are bought with a price: therefore glorify God in your body, and in your spirit, *which are God's* (I Cor. 6:19-20).

As a child of God by faith in Christ, I should consider the following: I really belong to God for He has purchased me out of the slave market of sin. Therefore He has every right to my life; and He really wants me to yield to Him so He can live through me. For that very purpose the Holy Spirit of God dwells within me. But God respects my free will and therefore I must choose to yield to Him, for He will not force me to live under His control. Not until I consciously and sincerely submit to His control, will the Holy Spirit fill my life with His power and influence. Not until I sincerely acknowledge His right to my life and act upon it by presenting myself completely to Him, will He take over. This submission includes my will, my desires, my ambitions, my choices, my whole being.

The New Testament presents a number of strong appeals to yield ourselves to God. "I beseech you therefore, brethren, by the mercies of God, that ye *present* your bodies a living sacrifice, holy, acceptable unto God, which is your reasonable service" (Rom. 12:1). "Neither yield ye your members as instruments of unrighteousness unto sin; but *yield* yourselves unto God, as those that are alive from the dead . . . ." (Rom. 6:13). The words "present" in 12:1, and "yield" in 6:13 are translations of the same word in the Greek text.

The opposite of yielding is resisting. That is why the Word admonishes believers: "Quench not the Spirit" (I Thess. 5:19). When the Spirit leads us in any way, we dare not put Him down.

The shortest sermon I ever listened to was also one of the most effective. In the early 1940s I served as a part-time teacher in the Washington Bible Institute (now Washington Bible College). At a graduation banquet one spring, the late Louis Sperry Chafer had been called from Dallas to be the special speaker. As often happens on such occasions, there were so many funny stories and responses, that it was after 10:00 p.m. when Dr. Chafer was finally introduced. He walked to the microphone and said something like this:

I had prepared a somewhat lengthier message, but the hour is late and I will not detain you. Therefore I am going to present just the three point outline of the message and let the Holy Spirit speak to us out of that outline. My subject is: The reasonableness of fully surrendering our lives to God. Reason No. 1: Because He is all-wise and knows better than anyone else what is best for my life. Reason No. 2: He is almighty and has the power to accomplish that which is best for me. Reason No. 3: He loves me more than anyone else in the world loves me. Conclusion: Therefore, the most logical thing the Christian can do is to surrender his life completely to God. What more can I say? What more need I say?

III. The Results of Being Filled with the Spirit

An entire book could well be written on the results of being filled with the Spirit since it covers the entire range of the believer's life and service. In this lesson we will consider only four of the major results.

A. The Spirit will make Christ real to the believer. We need to remember that the work of the Holy Spirit in this age is Christo-centric. His purpose is to reveal and to glorify Christ. Jesus said of the Spirit and His work: ". . . He shall not speak of himself . . . . He shall glorify me: for he shall receive of mine, and shall shew it unto you" (John 16:13-14). We may be sure that when the Holy Spirit fills our lives, Christ will become more real and more precious day by day. To be filled with the Spirit will result in falling in love with the Saviour all over again, until His love and His cause fills the life.

B. A Christ-like character will be formed. "But the fruit of the Spirit is love, joy, peace, longsuffering, gentleness, goodness, faith, meekness, temperance" (Gal. 5:22-23). This is the fruit of the Spirit; the wonderful result of His power and influence in the life that He fills. These are moral virtues and really present a description of the person of Christ in His humanity—God's perfect man. God's instruction to believers is: "For even hereunto were ye called; because Christ also suffered for us, leaving us an example, that ye should follow his steps" (I Peter 2:21). "Let this mind be in you, which was also in Christ Jesus . . . ." (Phil. 2:5).

C. I. Scofield has a note on Galatians 5:22-23 which says it much better than I can say it:

> Christian character is not mere moral or legal correctness, but the possession and manifestations of verses 22-23. Taken together they present a moral portrait of Christ, and may be understood as the apostle's explanation of 2:20, "Not I, but Christ," and as a definition of "fruit" in John 15:1-8. This character is possible because of the believer's vital union with Christ (John 15:5; I Cor. 12:12-13), and is wholly the fruit of the Spirit. "Fruit" (singular) in contrast with "works" (plural v. 19), suggests that

the Christian's life in the Spirit is unified in purpose and direction in contrast with the life in the flesh, with its inner conflicts and frustrations (The New Scofield Reference Bible, page 1270).

The believer who is filled with the Spirit will grow more and more like Christ. Consider the following breathtaking description: "But we all, with open face beholding as in a glass the glory of the Lord, are changed into the same image from glory to glory, even as *by the Spirit of the Lord*" (II Cor. 3:18). Permit me to quote Phillip's translation of this verse: "We are transfigured in ever increasing splendor into his own image, and the transformation comes from the Lord who is the Spirit."

> Let the beauty of Jesus be seen in me;
> All His wonderful passion and purity
> O thou Spirit divine, all my nature refine,
> Till the beauty of Jesus be seen in me.

C. The Spirit will give victory over the flesh, the sin-principle. "This I say then, Walk in the Spirit, and ye shall not fulfil the lust of the flesh" (Gal. 5:16). A more accurate translation would read: "Walk by means of the Spirit."

We have a lady in our congregation who walks by means of a walker. She is physically dependent upon that walker. Spiritually, we are to walk (live day by day) by means of, by the power of the Holy Spirit of God. This emphasizes the constant need of depending upon the Holy Spirit. That is the only way by which man can overcome the flesh, which is the old self. If we take one step in our own strength, we will fall on our faces.

D. He will give power for joyful service. "Out of his belly [out from within him] shall flow rivers of living water. (But this spake he of the Spirit, which they that believe on him should receive)" (John 7:38-39). "But ye shall receive power, after that the Holy Ghost is come upon you . . . ." (Acts 1:8). A careful reading of the first half of the Book of Acts will dramatically demonstrate the fulfillment of this promise. Following the phrases "filled with the Holy Ghost" and "full of the Holy Ghost" as found in 2:4; 4:8, 31; 6:3, 5; 7:55; 9:17; 11:24; and 13:9, 52, we discover that the source of the unstoppable power of the Early Church was the Holy Spirit who filled the lives of those first Christians. Ten times we are informed of such filling with the Spirit. As He filled their lives, men and women lived and served in His power. The resulting charm of their lives was so irresistible, the power of their witness for Christ was so convincing and persuasive, that there was a continuous succession of spiritual revivals.

Questions for Discussion:

1. How would you explain the difference between being indwelt by the Spirit, and being filled with the Spirit?

2. What is the real difference between a "carnal" and a "spiritual" Christian?

3. What are some of the prerequisites to being filled with the Spirit?

4. Which of the prerequisites is the most fundamental one?

5. What was the most obvious cause of the tremendous growth of the Early Church, as presented in the Book of Acts?

11

Romans 12:1-8; I Corinthians 12:4-11; Ephesians 4:11-16

The Gifts of the Holy Spirit

I. **The Meaning and Purpose of Spiritual Gifts in the Church**
   A. A definition
   B. The purpose of spiritual gifts
   C. These gifts are spiritual gifts.
   D. These gifts are gifts of grace.
   E. Having received a spiritual gift is no evidence of spirituality.
   F. Spiritual gifts must work together in harmony.
   G. Believers are exhorted to be diligent in the exercise of their spiritual gift or gifts.

Consideration of Individual Gifts

I. **Sign Gifts**

II. **Proclamation Gifts**
   A. Apostleship
   B. Prophecy
   C. Evangelism
   D. Pastoring
   E. Teaching
   F. Exhortation
   G. Knowledge, wisdom

III. **Service Gifts**
   A. Administration
   B. Ministering and helps
   C. Giving
   D. Showing mercy
   E. Faith
   F. Discernment

"Now concerning spiritual gifts, brethren, I would not have you ignorant" (I Cor. 12:1).

The church at Corinth was plagued with all kinds of spiritual problems, including strife and considerable confusion. Doubtless there were several causes for this, and their misunderstanding and misuse of spiritual gifts was certainly one of them, if not the main one. At least we find that Paul spent more time on the meaning and use of spiritual gifts than with any other subject in his first Epistle to the church. The apostle used 84 verses in our Bible, discussing the meaning, purpose, and proper use of spiritual gifts. Forty of those verses (all of chapter 14) deal with guidelines concerning the gift of speaking in tongues, a gift which was apparently misused most often by the Corinthian church.

There are at least seven different Greek words in the Greek New Testament which are translated "gift" or "gifts" in our English Bibles. However, the Greek word used when referring to the gifts of the Holy Spirit is *charisma,* which means "grace gift." From the Greek word *charisma* came the naming of the modern "Charismatic movement," which is a sweeping revival of interest in the gifts of the Spirit. As in the church at Corinth, today's movement with its tremendous emphasis on spiritual gifts, is accompanied by some disturbing misunderstandings and some misuses. The main problem rests upon a lack of differentiation between the sign gifts which were of temporary purpose (to authenticate the Gospel until the Scriptures were written), and the permanent gifts of the Spirit which are for believers throughout this present age of grace. Perhaps the best thing that has come out of the Charismatic movement is a renewed emphasis on the participation of the lay people of the church in the cause of Christ. This was long overdue, for one of the worst curses ever to strike the cause of Christ has been the elevation of the clergy as a select class in the church.

The purpose of this chapter is to present a brief survey of the Biblical meaning and purpose of spiritual gifts in general, and a short explanation of each of those gifts which are present in the Body of Christ today.

I. The Meaning and Purpose of Spiritual Gifts in the Church

A. A definition: As I understand it, a spiritual gift is the Holy Spirit's gift of special ability for the performance of Christian service within the Body of Christ. A more technical definition is found in Thayer's Greek-English Lexicon (p. 667) as follows: "Extraordinary powers, distinguishing certain Christians and enabling them to serve the church of Christ, the reception of which is due to the power of divine grace operating in their souls by the Holy Spirit."

B. The purpose of spiritual gifts is clearly stated in the New Testament, and centers in the edifying of the Body of Christ. "For the perfecting of the saints, for the work of the ministry, *for the edifying* of the body of Christ" (Eph. 4:12). "Even so ye, forasmuch as ye are zealous of spiritual gifts, seek that ye may excel *to the edifying of the church*" (I Cor. 14:12). ". . . Let all things be done *unto edifying*" (I Cor. 14:26).

"Edifying" in the New Testament means to promote or to contribute to the spiritual growth of the believers who constitute the Body of Christ. It is important that we understand this purpose, for it logically follows that any claimed gift of the Spirit which does not edify, or does in fact tear apart the Body of Christ, cannot be of the Holy Spirit.

C. These gifts are spiritual gifts, supernaturally bestowed by the Holy Spirit. They must therefore not be confused with natural talents. Spiritual gifts are the result of spiritual birth. Natural talents are the result of natural birth.

D. These gifts are gifts of grace (charis means "grace"). Therefore they are sovereignly bestowed by the Holy Spirit. They are in no way based upon human merit. "But all these worketh that one and the selfsame Spirit, dividing *to every man* severally *as he will*" (I Cor. 12:11). This also indicates that every believer has received at least one gift.

E. Having received a spiritual gift is no evidence of spirituality. Paul's first letter to the Corinthians indicates that they were richly endowed with spiritual gifts (cf. 1:5-7), yet they were carnal and used some of the gifts to further their own ambition. Commenting on this sad fact, Dr. W. A. Criswell wrote: "The gifts were mixed with human infirmity, and that sometime of the most reprehensible kind . . . . The gifts possessed by the saints were subject to frequent misuse: disorder, vanity, false ambition, exalted self-esteem, overweening egotism, personal superiority."

F. Although there is a variety of spiritual gifts, they must work together in harmony. "Now there are *diversities* of gifts, but *the same Spirit*" (I Cor. 12:4). As it takes many members to have a healthy physical body, each having its own particular function for the growth and well-being of that body, so in the Body of Christ. Although there are many gifts with different functions, they are all bestowed by the Holy Spirit and should certainly function in harmony toward the spiritual growth and well-being of the Body of Christ. This is the main message of I Corinthians 12. The admonition "That there should be no schism in the body; but that the members should have the same care one for another" (12:25) applies to the members in the use of their spiritual gifts. The spiritual growth and health of the Body is forever to be kept in mind in the use of the gifts. No doubt, spiritual gifts are sometimes used by Christians to attract attention to themselves, in order to shine (the Word calls it "vain glory"), or to make a name for themselves. But such is never the purpose of the Holy Spirit, for His gifts and such abuse will doubtless cause great embarrassment when we shall appear before the Bema seat of Christ.

G. Believers are exhorted to be diligent in the exercise of their spiritual gift or gifts. *"Neglect not the gift* that is in thee . . . ."* (I Tim. 4:14). "Wherefore I put thee in remembrance that thou *stir up the gift* of God, which is in thee by the putting on of my hands" (II Tim. 1:6). "As every man hath received the gift, even so *minister the same* one to another, as good stewards of the manifold grace of God" (I Peter 4:10).

We do not know what Timothy's spiritual gift was, but we do know that it was a *charisma*, for that is the word Paul used in speaking of it. But whatever the gift, Timothy is warned not to neglect it. He is also urged to "stir up" the gift. The Greek word which is translated "stir up" literally means to "fan the flame," like stirring up a fire. The opposite of this would be to let it die down through neglect, which Paul has warned against. After warning Timothy not to neglect the gift, Paul continues: "Meditate upon these things; give thyself wholly to them" (I Tim. 4:15).

Christian brother, Christian sister, God has given you a spiritual gift and He wants you to be diligent in exercising it. For many years I have been amazed at the casual attitude with which some preachers and teachers of the Word of God apply themselves to their God-given tasks! I am convinced that many a fair preacher would be a great preacher if he would only fan the flame of his spiritual gift. If 10 hours of diligent preparation will result in a good Sunday School lesson or sermon, 20 hours of prayerful work will produce a better one. But many pastors and teachers spend only two or three hours preparing for that all-important message or lesson of the week. And part of those few hours is often spent in daydreaming. Brethren, that is not giving ourselves wholly to it. The Holy Spirit does not give gifts to encourage laziness or neglect. I have not been able to find the "gift of gab" among the spiritual gifts. Along with Timothy, we must study to show ourselves approved unto God.

Consideration of Individual Gifts

There are various methods of listing spiritual gifts. I am dividing them in three groups, namely, Sign Gifts, Proclamation Gifts, and Service Gifts.

I. Sign Gifts

There are at least three spiritual gifts which were given to serve as "signs" or as God-given evidence to demonstrate that the messengers (apostles and evangelists) and the message which they brought before the New Testament existed, were of God. It is my understanding (after much study and prayer) that since their special purpose ended when the New Testament Scriptures were completed, these signs also ceased, or at least were greatly diminished. Inasmuch as the next chapter in this Study Guide will be devoted to a discussion of these sign gifts, they will not be treated here. The sign gifts are: A. the gift of miracles; B. the gift of healing; C. the gift of speaking in (unknown) tongues and the interpretation of tongues.

II. Proclamation Gifts

This list of gifts is sometimes called "the speaking gifts." These gifts are concerned with the oral proclamation of the Word of God.

A. The gift of apostleship (Eph. 4:11; cf. I Cor. 12:28). Both of these references speak of certain people being gifts to the church. Some of them were to function as apostles, others as prophets. An apostle is a specially appointed delegate of Christ who has received special authority and power. Some believe that both the office of an apostle and the gift of apostleship ceased when the original apostles were gone. Others insist that the gift continues today in the calling of a missionary. Though this view has some merit, it would be difficult to prove that all the original apostles were missionaries.

B. The gift of prophecy (Rom. 12:6; I Cor. 12:10, 28; 14:1, 4, 5; Eph. 2:20; 4:11). A. T. Robertson defines the ministry of a New Testament prophet as: "A speaking forth of God's message under the guidance of the Holy Spirit" (A. T. Robertson, *Word Pictures in the New Testament,* Vol. IV, p. 169). The first thought that comes to most of us when we hear the word "prophet" or "prophecy" is that of predicting what will happen in the future. Although prediction is sometimes a part of prophecy, it certainly is not the main function of the prophet.

From the Scriptures we learn that the gift of prophecy was received by both men and women (cf. Acts 21:8-9; I Cor. 11:5). This gift is ranked as being of primary importance doubtless because of its strong contribution to the spiritual growth of believers (cf. I Cor. 14:1, 3, 5, 19, 22).

Because God's revelation to man has been completed in the canon of the Scriptures, the function of the gift of prophecy is now limited to the Spirit-led function of expounding that revelation.

C. The gift of evangelism (Eph. 4:11, cf. Acts 21:8; II Tim. 4:5). The gift of evangelism is the God-given ability to effectively communicate the Gospel to the unsaved. Philip is the only person who is called an evangelist in the Bible. He was a deacon by office, but an evangelist by gift of the Holy Spirit. Timothy, who was a pastor by office, was exhorted to do the work of an evangelist—present the Gospel to the unsaved.

D. The gift of pastoring (Eph. 4:11). The Greek word translated "pastor" is *poimen* and is translated 15 times "shepherd"; and "pastor" only in this verse. The pastor *is* a shepherd. This means that he is to care for the spiritual well-being of the congregation. He is to feed, guide, and train the members of the Body of Christ. This is no small task, and to be thus gifted by the Holy Spirit is greatly desired. It seems that because of the complexity and energy-demanding work involved, many are leaving the pastorate today for other avenues of service. W. A. Criswell says: "A worthy pastor is a true gift from heaven."

E. The gift of teaching (Rom. 12:7; I Cor. 12:28-29; Eph. 4:11). The gift of teaching is the God-given ability to so explain the Word of God that believers will be equipped and inspired for Christian service, encouraged to study the Word for themselves, ready to share the Lord with others, and be fortified against false teachers and their doctrines. In my opinion, this is the gift that is needed most in our churches today.

F. The gift of exhortation (Rom. 12:8). This is one of the least known and appreciated, but tremendously valuable gifts of the Spirit. The Greek word for it is *paraklesis*, and the Holy Spirit is called the *Parakleton* by Christ, which is translated "the Comforter" in our Bible. The gift of exhortation is the God-given ability to comfort, to encourage, to reassure and strengthen new converts and those who are weak or discouraged. Blessed is the congregation which has several so-gifted persons. The outstanding example of a person with this gift is Joses, who because of this wonderful ability was nicknamed by the apostles "Barnabas" (Acts 4:36). Freely interpreted, the word "Barnabas" is the equivalent of our "big brother." We discover that Barnabas encouraged or exhorted:

A new convert who was under suspicion (Acts 9:26-28).

A new congregation that was being investigated (Acts 11:19-24).

A very gifted, but unused teacher (Acts 11:25-26).

A young missionary who had failed (Acts 15:35-39).

How I thank God for a few big brothers and big sisters in my life to whom God had given the gift of exhortation! Without their encouragement I might have quit the ministry to which God had called me.

G. The gift of knowledge and of wisdom (I Cor. 12:8). These two gifts are closely related and so I am presenting them together. The gift of knowledge has to do with the understanding of spiritual truth. The "*word* of knowledge" speaks of the ability to communicate the truth to others.

The gift of wisdom is the special ability to *apply* spiritual truth in a practical way for spiritual profit. This gift is especially helpful in the field of spiritual counseling. There is a wonderful description of the wisdom which the Holy Spirit gives in James 3:17.

III. Service Gifts

There are a number of spiritual gifts that relate to special abilities in Christian service, which do not necessarily involve public speaking—such as giving, showing mercy, and so forth.

A. The gift of administration. "He that ruleth [let him do so], with diligence" (Rom. 12:8). "God hath set some in the church . . . governments" (I Cor. 12:28). Dr. Criswell speaks of this gift as "the ability to guide the church through all the fortunes and vicissitudes of daily life, maintaining order and holding the congregation to its heavenly assignment." As the shepherd, the pastor often has to act as the administrator as well. But not many pastors have this ability as a special gift of the Spirit. Others in the congregation may possess such a gift. The exhortation is that in all cases the gift must be exercised with diligence.

B. The gifts of ministering (Rom. 12:7) and helps (I Cor. 12:28). The Greek word for "ministering" is *diakonia* and so could well be called the gift of "deaconing." Both ministering and helps speak of the special ability to aid others in Christian love. This is certainly a wide-open field and happy is the pastor who finds several so-gifted persons in his congregation. Dr. Gangel makes this thought-provoking comment: "Very few cults grow up around the people who exercise the gift of helps."

C. The gift of giving. "He that giveth, let him do it with simplicity" (Rom. 12:8). Giving with simplicity is a God-given gift. At another time and place the apostle called it a "grace" (II Cor. 8:7). The idea of giving with simplicity is to give with cheerful generosity, remembering that "God loveth a cheerful giver" (II Cor. 9:7). The gift of giving is the God-given ability to use one's means wisely and joyously for the glory of God.

D. The gift of showing mercy (Rom. 12:8). This is the important and much-needed ability to exercise genuine Christian sympathy to those who are hurting. After a visit, if those who are hurting are left in better spirits, there is evidence of someone who has shown a real gift of God, involving both love and wisdom.

We have a Christian lady in our congregation who visits several rest homes every Sunday afternoon to spend a little time with those lonely people there who are seldom, or never visited by anyone else. She knows their problems and the things they enjoy, and usually takes them a small present. She also shares her Saviour with them. She genuinely loves them. Needless to say, they look forward all week long to her coming. She exercises her gift with cheerfulness.

E. The gift of faith (I Cor. 12:9). This wonderful gift is the God-given ability to believe God can and will do what most of us, who are so practical, consider impossible. In reality, those who fully believe God are the practical ones. After all, if God is what we say He is (and He is even more than that) we ought to trust Him to do what ought to be done according to His will, no matter how unlikely it may appear to the natural mind. There is nothing that delights the heart of God more than when His children simply and completely trust Him for great things. The sigh of disappointment from our Lord was: "O, ye of *little* faith"! Fortunately, there are still those who have the gift of faith.

F. The gift of discernment (I Cor. 12:10). The gift of "discerning of spirits" is the God-given ability to tell truth from error, to detect the false that hides under the pretense of truth, in spiritual teaching and preaching. Leslie B. Flynn says that the person with this gift has "the ability to spot a phony before others see through his phoniness."

The gift of discernment was especially needed in the Early Church, since there was no written revelation outside of the Old Testament, to appeal to in deciding between truth and error. In our time this gift is again needed for the testing of the message *by* the written Word of God. Satan has his counterfeit for everything spiritual. He and his assistants are very clever in hiding a little bit of error under a great deal of truth, knowing that "a little leaven leaveneth the whole lump." The inspired warning of John seems to be especially pertinent for our time: "Beloved, believe not every spirit, but try the spirits whether they be of God: because many false prophets are gone out into the world" (I John 4:1).

Spiritual Gifts and Love

"... And yet shew I unto you a more excellent way" (I Cor. 12:31). Perhaps the most important thing to be said about spiritual gifts is that all of them must be administered IN LOVE. This is the "more excellent way." This is the burden of chapter 13 of I Corinthians, and the very center of Paul's long discourse on spiritual gifts. Unfortunately, the Authorized Version has "charity" instead of love. The central truth all through the chapter is that without true Christian love, all Christian service (no matter how gifted) is worthless.

We must not miss the mention of spiritual gifts in the thirteenth chapter. "Though I speak with the *tongues* of men and of angels .... And though I have *the gift of prophecy,* and *understand* all mysteries, and all *knowledge*; and though I have all faith .... And though I *bestow all my goods* to feed the poor ...." (13:1-3). These are spiritual gifts. Without the ingredient of true love, they are hollow. It is the very love of God shed abroad in our hearts by the Holy Ghost—that real, true, unselfish love, that fulfills the purpose of spiritual gifts. It will help us to understand the whole if we remember that Paul did not divide his Epistle by chapters. Chapter divisions are not inspired and sometimes becloud the issue.

Yes, love is the more excellent way. Love gives power to teaching and preaching. It gives warmth to mercy and ministering. Love adds strength to exhortation and joy to giving. Love makes administration agreeable and gives meaning to the whole purpose of spiritual gifts, which is the building up of the Body of Christ. Without this ingredient of true love, spiritual gifts will soon make us proud and critical of others. The greatest thing is love, for love "never faileth" (I Cor. 13:8).

Conclusions:

1. The Holy Spirit has given one or more spiritual gifts to every Christian.

2. The Lord wants us to recognize and then exercise our gifts with great earnestness.

3. The purpose of all spiritual gifts today is to promote the spiritual growth of the Body of Christ, that in turn will result in numerical increase as well.

4. Above all, spiritual gifts must always be exercised in love.

Questions for Discussion:

1. What is the difference between spiritual gifts and natural talents?

2. According to Ephesians 4:12 and I Corinthians 14:12, what is the real purpose for spiritual gifts in the church today?

3. Can you explain the meaning of the gift of exhortation?

4. Why is love so important in the use of all spiritual gifts?

12

I Corinthians 14:1-40

The Sign Gifts

I. **These Gifts Are Sign Gifts**
   A. Confirmation
   B. Promise
   C. Purpose

II. **The Biblical Background of Miracles as Signs**
   A. Moses
   B. Elijah
   C. Jesus Christ
   D. The apostles and evangelists
   E. The two witnesses of God

III. **The Gift of Working Miracles**
   A. A display of supernatural power
   B. The *gift* apparently ceased or became very rare.

IV. **The Gift of Healing**
   A. Divine healing for today
   B. A difference between divine healing and the gift of healing
   C. God's will about illness
   D. Illness and sin
   E. The practice of faith-healing
   F. Does the gift of healing exist today?

V. **The Gift of Tongues**
   A. Involves a miracle
   B. A sign gift
   C. A gift of the Holy Spirit
   D. An inferior gift
   E. In public worship
   F. Guard against division within the Body of Christ.
   G. A gift for all believers?
   H. Is the gift of tongues for today?

". . . after that miracles, then gifts of healings . . . diversity of tongues" (I Cor. 12:28).

Miracles, gifts of healings, diversity of tongues—these are highly controversial subjects among Christians today. After reading many books on the subject, my reaction was a great desire to pass the matter by. But that would not be true to the purpose of a "Study Guide." Furthermore, if we should avoid all subjects that are controversial, we would not have much to teach or preach. Although well aware of the fact that I am not an expert or an authority on these subjects, I have unquestioning faith in the veracity and authority of God's Word. Therefore, without malice toward any but with love toward all who love my Saviour, I shall try to present what I believe the Bible teaches on the gifts of miracles, healings, and the speaking in tongues.

I. These Gifts Are Sign Gifts

Sign gifts are supernatural manifestations through human agency, signifying God's public endorsement of both His messenger and the message that he brings.

A. Christ had promised to confirm His messengers and their message with supernatural signs.

> And he said unto them, Go ye into all the world, and preach the gospel to every creature . . . . And *these signs* shall follow them that believe; in my name shall they cast out devils; they shall speak with new tongues; they shall take up serpents; and if they drink any deadly thing, it shall not hurt them; they shall lay hands on the sick, and they shall recover . . . . (Mark 16:15-18).

Three different signs were promised by our Lord: namely, miracles (such as casting out devils, prevention from harm in case of poisoning); speaking with new tongues; and healing of the sick. About 20 years later the Apostle Paul wrote: "Wherefore *tongues are for a sign,* not to them that believe, but to them that believe not . . . ." (I Cor. 14:22).

B. The promise of signs was certainly fulfilled. "And they went forth, and preached every where, the Lord working with them, and *confirming the word with signs* following" (Mark 16:20). ". . . And many wonders and signs were done by the apostles" (Acts 2:43). "And by the hands of the apostles were many *signs and wonders* wrought among the people . . . ." (Acts 5:12). ". . . beholding the *miracles and signs* which were done" (Acts 8:13). "Long time therefore abode they speaking boldly *in the Lord, which gave testimony unto the word of his grace,* and granted *signs and wonders* to be done by their hands" (Acts 14:3). "Truly *the signs of an apostle* were wrought among you in all patience, in *signs, and wonders,* and mighty deeds" (II Cor. 12:12).

The Book of Acts documents the fulfillment of the signs that Jesus had promised. Many miracles were performed by the apostles. The phenomena of speaking in different tongues on the Day of Pentecost was the *first* sign confirming the new message of the Gospel.

C. The purpose of these signs was to publicly demonstrate God's approval of the messenger and his message. By means of these supernatural signs, God declared that the person through whom the miracle was wrought was God's appointed messenger and that his message was the message of God Himself. "And they went forth, and preached every where, the Lord working with them, and *confirming the word with signs* following" (Mark 16:20).

For the first two decades after Pentecost there was no written New Testament at all. The disciples began to proclaim the fantastic news that Jesus of Nazareth was the Son of God who had died for the sins of the world, that He had risen from the grave and was alive, and that all who received Him would be saved. They insisted that this was God's message. But where was their credential, their authority? Then the Lord worked with them and "confirmed" their claims. He backed them up with supernatural events that served as signs of His approval. "God also bearing them witness, both with signs and wonders, and with divers miracles, and gifts of the Holy Ghost, according to his own will" (Heb. 2:4).

II. The Biblical Background of Miracles as Signs

The Scriptures record five periods in the history of God's dealings with man on earth in which a series of public miracles was used (or will be used). In each case they serve as signs of God's approval of certain messengers and their message. These periods and the messengers involved are:

A. Moses, at the time of Israel's redemption from the bondage of Egypt. "He [Moses] brought them out, after that he had shewed wonders and signs in the land of Egypt, and in the Red sea, and in the wilderness forty years" (Acts 7:36). The fact that the miracles which Moses performed were actually signs from God is mentioned 11 times in the Book of Exodus (cf. Ex. 4:28, 30; 10:1-2).

B. Elijah, at the time of Israel's great apostacy. At the time of the great test by fire on Mt. Carmel, Elijah prayed: "Lord God of Abraham, Isaac, and of Israel, let it be known this day that thou art God in Israel, and *that I am thy servant*, and that I have done all these things *at thy word*" (I Kings 18:36). Of course, God wonderfully confirmed Elijah and his message with fire from heaven in the sight of all the people.

C. Jesus Christ, during the three years of His public ministry. "Ye men of Israel, hear these words; Jesus of Nazareth, a man *approved of God among you* by *miracles* and *wonders* and *signs,* which God did by him in the midst of you . . . ." (Acts 2:22; cf. John 20:31). The many supernatural deeds which Jesus performed were signs or proofs of His deity. They also served to bear witness to His claim that He had been sent by the Father and that His message was the message of God.

D. The apostles and evangelists, during the apostolic period. Almost every page of the first half of the Book of Acts reports one or more miracles. "And fear came upon every soul; and many wonders and signs were done by the apostles" (2:43). "And by the hands of the apostles were

many signs and wonders wrought among the people . . . ."
(5:12; cf. 5:16; 6:8; 8:6-7).

E. The two witnesses of God, during the coming Great Tribulation.

> And I will give power unto my two witnesses . . . . These have power to shut heaven, that it rain not in the days of their prophecy: and have power over waters to turn them to blood, and to smite the earth with all plagues, as often as they will. And when they shall have finished their testimony, the beast . . . shall overcome them, and kill them (Rev. 11:3-7).

There are at least three things that all five of these eruptions or miracles have in common. (1) They are performed in public. (2) They are performed in an atmosphere of unbelief. (3) They serve as signs to confirm the messengers and the message.

III. The Gift of Working Miracles

"To another [is given] the working of miracles . . . ." (I Cor. 12:10; cf. v. 28).

A. The Biblical word "miracle" signifies a display of supernatural power such as Jesus used on many occasions. The *gift* of working miracles is God's gift to man to perform a miracle. There are miracles today, and I have witnessed some of them. God's power has not lessened. But in the days of the apostles, certain men had the gift from God to perform miracles. Paul pronounced immediate blindness upon the sorcerer Elymas who tried to keep the deputy Sergius Paulus from obeying the Gospel. Elymas immediately was struck with blindness, and the deputy "When he saw what was done, believed . . . ." (Acts 13:12). Peter prayed and then addressed the corpse that had been Dorcas, and commanded: "Tabitha, arise" (Acts 9:40). The record reports: "And she opened her eyes . . . . And it was known throughout all Joppa; and many believed in the Lord" (Acts 9:40-42). Paul insisted that his many miracles were signs of his apostleship (cf. II Cor. 12:12).

B. The gift of working miracles apparently ceased or became very rare at the close of the apostolic period. For emphasis I repeat that I do not mean that miracles ceased. Our God is a God of miracles. But *the special gift to man to work miracles* ceased as far as I can determine.

There are several reasons for believing that the gift of working miracles ceased. One good reason is that the need and purpose for this gift no longer existed with the completion of the New Testament. Until the New Testament was written, the gift of working miracles served to authenticate the message. This message was also new revelation. Once the new revelation was completed and documented, this revelation became the authority of the messengers. If some have the idea that miracles would turn people to Christ even though they do not believe the Scriptures, the statement which Jesus put in the mouth of Abraham in Paradise should disillusion them: "If they hear not Moses and the prophets, neither will they be persuaded, though one rose from the dead" (Luke 16:31).

IV. The Gift of Healing

"To another the gifts of healing" (I Cor. 12:9; cf. vv. 28, 30).

Within the Biblical context, the gift of healing is the God-given power to procure instantaneous deliverance from physical and mental illnesses, in the name of the Lord. This gift was certainly one of the promised signs of the Lord: "They shall lay hands on the sick, and they shall recover" (Mark 16:18). The Book of Acts records many usages of this gift, beginning with the healing of the man who was lame from his birth (cf. 3:2-8).

There is hardly a more controversial subject among Christians these days than that of divine healing. Thousands of professional faith-healers are active in America and Europe. Many of them are doing a big business and are prospering financially from their professed gift. There are doubtless many things that I don't know about the subject of divine healing, and one should not talk (and certainly not write) concerning what he does not know. I will therefore confine myself to that which I do know and believe from searching God's Word.

A. Yes, I certainly do believe in divine healing for today. I have been a witness to some such healings during 43 years in the Christian ministry. All the miraculous healings that I know anything about came in answer to fervent prayer, often involving whole congregations. The Holy Spirit has given us some definite instructions on what believers ought to do, in the realm of the spiritual, when they become ill. These instructions are found in chapter 5 of the Epistle of James, verses 13-16. The God whom we serve is able to heal and He delights in answering the prayers of His children.

B. There is a real difference between divine healing in answer to prayer, and the gift of healing. The gift was granted to the apostles and at least two of the early evangelists to attest their mission and their message. They used this gift abundantly. The effectiveness of this gift was in no way dependent upon the faith of the person to be healed. Consider the first use of the gift by Peter as recorded in Acts 3:2-8 as a classic example: The poor cripple was looking for a donation from Peter and John. He had no idea of who they were or of experiencing a miracle. The need for believing was never mentioned. Instead of giving a donation, Peter commanded: "In the name of Jesus Christ of Nazareth rise up and walk . . . . and immediately his feet and ankle bones received strength." As a result he was "walking, and leaping, and praising God." We may rest assured that the lame man was the most surprised person present.

C. It is not true that it is not God's will that any of His children be ill. Nor has God promised that believers would be delivered from all physical illnesses in this life. There are tremendous spiritual changes when a person is born again. But getting sick, suffering pain, being tempted, getting old, and dying are still his lot, the same as with the unsaved. Paul said it rather dramatically:

> For we know that the whole creation groaneth and travaileth in pain together until now. And *not only they, but ourselves also,* which have the firstfruits of the Spirit, even we ourselves groan within ourselves, waiting for the adoption, to wit, the redemption of our body (Rom. 8:22-23).

Our complete deliverance from illnesses awaits the resurrection at the coming of the Lord. In the meantime, believers (including faith-healers) are subject to the same viruses, accidents, aches and pains, aging processes, and so forth, as are others.

D. It is not true that when believers become ill, it is always because there is sin in their lives. It is not personal judgment. This is an old superstition that Jesus faced and unmasked in His day (John 9:1-4). Paul had an infirmity and prayed to be delivered from it. But the Lord said Paul should bear and use it for the glory of God. We read in the Word about teachers and preachers being ill, without a word being said about there being sin in their lives. For example: Timothy (I Tim. 5:23); Epaphroditus, who became ill because of overwork in the service of the Lord (Phil. 2:25-30); and Trophimus, whom Paul had to leave behind in a state of illness (II Tim. 4:20). Having the gift of healing, why didn't Paul heal those friends? The only reason I can come up with is that it was not God's will that they be healed miraculously.

E. The practice of faith-healing for financial gain is so completely foreign to the Scriptures and to the very nature of Christianity that it is an insult to the intelligence of true believers.

F. What about the question: Does the gift of healing exist today? Believing in the sovereignty of the Holy Spirit, I do not see why He could not bestow the gift upon a servant of God, in special situations, where a purpose for the gift would exist. Such might be the case in missionary endeavor in remote areas where primitive people are not able to read the

Scriptures. Without being dogmatic about it, I believe that where the Word of God is available the special gift of the Holy Spirit to perform instant healings has ceased. Or at least this gift is very rare since the completion of the New Testament. This conclusion is based upon two Biblical evidences: (1) The gift of healing is one of the sign gifts where the stated purpose was to confirm God's messengers and their message. This new message was also new revelation. (2) All the miracles of healing reported after Pentecost are to be found in the Book of Acts. Illnesses are reported in the Epistles, but not a single instant cure through the gift of healing is to be found after Acts 28. The only report of miraculous healing reported in the 22 books after Acts is the apparent healing of the "beast" from his "deadly wound" (cf. Rev. 13:3). This is still in the future and apparently is satanic as to its source of power.

V. The Gift of Tongues

"They shall speak with new tongues" (Mark 16:17). ". . . To another divers kinds of tongues; to another the interpretation of tongues" (I Cor. 12:10; cf. v. 28).

The issue of tongues is a problem in many churches today. However, this is not the first time that it has been a problem in a congregation. Tongues were a real problem in the church at Corinth, and Paul tried hard to deal with the problem. It is well for us to note before we begin a study of the subject, that Paul, while giving definite instructions concerning the use of the gift of tongues, stated that these instructions were "the commandments of the Lord" (I Cor. 14:37).

While mine won't be the last words on the subject, I suggest the following observations:

A. The gift of speaking in tongues involves a miracle as with the gift of healing. At least on the Day of Pentecost the manifestation of the gift involved speaking in languages which the apostles had not learned. This is a miracle, as everyone who has ever tried to learn a foreign language will be quick to acknowledge. I realize that some Bible scholars hold that even at Pentecost no real languages were involved. But this is difficult for me to accept when I read that the people present from many foreign countries said: ". . . We do *hear them speak in our own tongues* the wonderful works of God" (Acts 2:11). They also said: "Behold, are not all these which speak Galilaeans? And how hear we every man in our own tongue, wherein we were born?" (vv. 7-8). Now if I said that I heard a man praise God in my mother tongue, it would mean that I heard him speak in German, for that is the language in which *I* was born. It would mean that he spoke intelligibly and that I understood what he said in German, because if this were not the case, I would not know that he was speaking the wonderful works of God.

Ecstatic utterances they may have been, if by that we mean their utterances were words of praise. But the apostles were uttering the praises in foreign languages, and those who heard them speak understood what they said. This is really the point in the whole report. The desired result was produced, for the people asked: "What meaneth this?" (2:12), which gave Peter the opportunity to proclaim the gospel of salvation by faith in Christ for the first time to a large audience. This proclamation was not in a foreign language (in which case only some would have understood), but in the language which all Jews understood.

Whether the speaking in tongues as practiced in Corinth also involved real languages, I do not know. Many writers believe that the speaking in tongues in that congregation consisted of ecstatic utterances in sounds that none understood except the person who had the gift of interpretation. Some of the things Paul said about it seem to support that view. The tongues spoken at Pentecost were understood. The tongues practiced in Corinth were understood by no one (cf. I Cor. 14:2).

B. The speaking in tongues is a sign gift. It was so promised by our Lord: "And these signs shall follow them that believe . . . they shall speak with new tongues" (Mark 16:17). The apostle declared: "Wherefore tongues are for a sign . . . ." (I Cor. 14:22).

C. Perhaps the most important fact about the gift of tongues is that it is the gift of the Holy Spirit (when it is real). We read that on the Day of Pentecost they "began to speak with other tongues, *as the Spirit gave them utterance*" (Acts 2:4). This being so, there cannot be anything wrong with what is said and with how it is said, *unless* the flesh can replace the Spirit in the use of the gift.

Dr. James Boyer has stated in *Studies in I Corinthians* the significance of this forcefully and logically as follows:

> The second crucial characteristic of tongues-speaking at Corinth was that something was wrong with it. Here is a very important yet little understood factor in this problem. The gift of tongues in Corinth was being misused, and Paul wrote to correct and regulate its proper use. It was being rated too highly. It was being used excessively. It was contributing to disorder and confusion. Above all, it was useless for edifying. But he makes no hint that it was spurious or pretended. Now the necessary implication is that it could not have been miraculous, in the sense that it was the direct working of God which enabled them to speak in tongues, else God was misusing the gift. If they could speak in tongues only as God gave them to speak, then when many of them caused confusion by speaking at one time it was really God causing the confusion by performing many miracles of speaking at one time; and so with the other abuses. If speaking in tongues was the ability to speak a foreign language not previously learned, then it was a miraculous power which could be performed only when God enabled, and could not be performed by more than one at a time unless God did it. It is simply impossible to conceive of the misuse of a totally miraculous gift. The conclusion seems inescapable: The gift of tongues was an ability which was capable of being used and controlled miraculously by God for His purposes, and was also capable of being used and controlled by the individual for unworthy and improper purposes. The problem at Corinth was the exercise of this gift in the power of the flesh instead of the power of God.

D. The gift of tongues is an inferior gift. This is evident from Paul's way of dealing with tongues. We notice that he places it at the bottom of the list of spiritual gifts, followed only by the gift of interpretation of tongues, in I Corinthians 12:8-10. According to the apostle, the gift of tongues did not edify the church, but the speaker only (14:2-5), and because it did not edify the Body of Christ, it was of little importance.

E. Paul insisted that everything that goes on in public worship be intelligible (cf. I Cor. 14:6-9, 18-20). A careful reading of these verses should convince anyone that the apostle disapproved of speaking in tongues in public services. He would permit it only if an interpreter was present who could tell the people what was said. The reason behind the disapproval evidently was that it did not contribute anything to the spiritual growth of believers, the Body of Christ. This is both logical and understandable.

A gospel song with a spiritual message really lifts me up, whether sung by the congregation, choir, quartet, trio, duet or by a soloist, *providing* I can understand the words that tell the message. When I cannot understand the words, it means nothing to me, no matter how perfect the lyrics. This is what Paul is saying about tongues as practiced among the Corinthians.

F. The main thrust of Paul in the instructions concerning spiritual gifts is to guard against division within the Body of Christ. This is the central plea of all 84 verses in chapters 12 to 14 of I Corinthians. This purpose is often repeated for emphasis (14:3-4, 12, 17, 26). "To edify" means "to build up, to strengthen." Is it too much to conclude that anything that tears apart the Body of Christ is not of the Holy Spirit, but of the flesh?

G. The assertion that the gift of speaking in tongues belongs to all believers, is totally unbiblical. "Are all apostles? . . . are all workers of miracles? Have all the gifts of healing? do all speak with tongues? Do all interpret?" (I Cor.

12:29-30). These are all rhetorical questions which demand a negative answer. Are all apostles? Of course not. Not all have the gift of healing. Nor do all speak with tongues.

H. The question remains: Is the gift of tongues for today? The apostle makes two statements which seem to be opposed to each other. First he says: "Charity [love] never faileth . . . whether there be tongues, *they shall cease*" (I Cor. 13:8). A bit later he sums up the whole discussion on the gift of tongues with: "Wherefore, brethren, covet to prophesy, and *forbid not to speak with tongues.* Let all things be done decently and in order" (14:39-40). The apparent difficulty is cleared up when we remember that the sign gifts were to function until the new revelation was completed in written form. This letter to the Corinthians is one of the earlier books of the New Testament, written when very few of the other books existed. At that time the sign gifts were still functioning though already diminishing. To forbid speaking in tongues at that time would have been limiting the Holy Spirit.

My own conviction concerning the appearance of the gift of tongues today is this: knowing that the Holy Spirit is sovereign and almighty, I have no right to declare dogmatically that He will never grant the Biblical gift of speaking in other tongues to anyone today or in the future. But precisely because He is the Holy Spirit, I am certain He will not give the gift in contradiction to the instructions which He gave concerning the use of the gift in His Word. In other words, I believe that where tongues are used in a manner openly contradictory to God's Word, they are not the gift of the Holy Spirit. This is not an arbitrary nor unkind statement, but the only possible conclusion that fits the infallibility of the Scriptures and the faithfulness of God.

Practical Applications:

A. There is a great need for the constant and Spirit-led presentation (in understandable words) of all the counsel of

God in our churches today. This calls for careful and prayerful study of the Scriptures.

B. The work of the shepherd is to care for the sheep and to guard them against danger. Pastors therefore should guard against the intrusion of teachers and teachings that tend toward divisiveness.

C. We should promote and seek to provide an atmosphere of love and joyful fellowship in our churches in which all can participate. We should also strive to encourage all the members of the Body to participate in the great work of building up the Body of Christ.

D. Let us place proper emphasis on the fruit of the Spirit, which is the evidence of spirituality and the result of being filled with the Spirit.

E. In the spirit of Christian love we should ask our Pentecostal brethren to avoid pressing their views on the gift of tongues on other believers. The Holy Spirit's mission and goal is to magnify Christ and to build up His Body, not to hurt it.

Questions for Discussion:

1. What is the "gift of working miracles"?
2. How did miracles serve as "signs" in the days of the apostles?
3. What is the difference between divine healing and the "gifts of healing"?
4. Was the gift of healing dependent upon the faith of the sick?
5. Can the gift of speaking in tongues be expressed contrary to the regulations laid down in I Corinthians chapter 14?

13

Ephesians 4:18-32

Sinning against
the Holy Spirit of God

I. The Sin of Lying to the Holy Spirit
   A. The question naturally arises, were Ananias and Sapphira saved?
   B. Their sin was spiritual hypocrisy.
   C. Their lie before the church was lying to the Holy Spirit.

II. The Sin of Grieving the Holy Spirit
   A. We grieve the Holy Spirit by corrupt speech.
   B. The Holy Spirit is grieved by an unchristian attitude toward others.
   C. Murmuring and complaining will grieve the Holy Spirit.

III. The Sin of Quenching the Holy Spirit

The Holy Spirit is a very important person in the believer's life. He plays the most significant role in a person's salvation, from start to finish. In a very real sense the Holy Spirit is to spiritual life what a mother is to the child's physical life. The mother brings the child into life, nourishes, cares for, trains, and watches over him with sacrificial love. She also has high hopes and great ambitions for her child. Even so, the Holy Spirit brings the believer into spiritual life and into the family of God. He indwells the believer, nourishes him, cares for him, guides, reproves, and strengthens him in true love. The Spirit also has great expectations for each believer.

Now, a mother can be made glad or sad by the attitude and behavior of her child. She can be grieved, defeated, and deceived by her child. The hurt is all the greater because of the love that is in her heart. The Holy Spirit can be lied to, grieved, and stymied in His love and power, by the attitude and behavior of the believer. And as with the mother, the hurt is all the greater because each member of the Body of Christ is dear to Him.

The various ways in which the believer may offend the Holy Spirit are summed up in God's Word under three headings. We call them the sins against the Holy Spirit.

I. The Sin of Lying to the Holy Spirit

"But Peter said, Ananias, why hath Satan filled thine heart to lie to the Holy Ghost . . . . thou hast not lied unto men, but unto God" (Acts 5:3-4).

The young church was growing by leaps and bounds, and Satan did not like it at all. He tried to stop the growth by persecution, but that seemed only to increase the fervor of the Christians. Therefore Satan tried to work from within the church. Knowing from long experience that man's weak side is his pride—the desire to shine—and that this desire can usually be guided into unholy ambitions, Satan sought, and found the opportunity to use this weakness in the church at Jerusalem.

Barnabas, a deeply spiritual man, had recently sold his real estate holdings on the island of Cyprus and had brought the whole proceeds to the apostles to be used in the Lord's work. Somehow the news of this leaked out and people talked about this wonderful generosity. This was Satan's opportunity!

Ananias and Sapphira were new Christians. All that fuss over Barnabas created a bit of envy in their hearts. This was natural. Satan worked on that and then planted the idea in their hearts that they could sell their property, put away part of the proceeds for a rainy day, and bring the remainder to the apostles. It wouldn't really hurt to let the apostles think that they had given the whole amount of the sale.

The devil planted the thought. The desire for recognition received the seed. It conceived and brought forth the sin, and sin brought forth death. They lied and died. What concerns us most about the incident is the fact that Peter said they had lied to the Holy Spirit. This incident holds some very important truths for believers today.

A. The question naturally arises, were Ananias and Sapphira saved? I believe they were saved, though none of us can be certain about this. The fact that their sin was judged indicates they were members of God's family. This reasoning is based upon such Scriptures as I Corinthians 5:4-5 and 11:29-32. Theirs was a token judgment which demonstrated God's estimate of sin and served as a warning for this entire age—God judges sin. When Israel entered the Promised Land, God judged the first sin of covetousness committed by Achan (Joshua, chap. 7). God likewise made an example of this sin at the beginning of the church to demonstrate for all time how serious it is to trifle with the Holy Spirit of God. If the Lord would judge the same sin in the same swift manner in the church today, there would not be many Christians alive, or many pastors left to lead them. But God still feels exactly the same about sin as He did in the days of the apostles.

B. Their sin was spiritual hypocrisy. Keeping back part of the money was not sin, as Peter so carefully pointed out in the Acts passage. All giving must be voluntary to be giving in the sight of God. They pretended before the church that they had given the whole amount, which was a lie. This lie was acted out by Ananias and later put into words by Sapphira.

C. Their lie before the church was lying to the Holy Spirit. This fact involves a very important principle—that is, any pretending or lying in spiritual matters that is done to impress the church, is pretense or lying to the Holy Spirit. It is the same principle as that which is seen in the words of Christ to Saul of Tarsus: "Saul, Saul, why persecutest thou *me*?" (Acts 9:4). Christ and His Church and the Holy Spirit and Christ's Church are all one. Therefore, hurting the Church is hurting Christ and lying to the Church is lying to the Holy Spirit. We note that when Peter told Ananias that he had lied to the Holy Spirit, he added that he had lied to God. Any attack against His people, the Lord regards as an attack against His person. Any spiritual pretense before His people is pretense before God.

Considering this principle seriously will very likely bring conviction and a new appreciation of God's patience to our hearts. How do believers commit the sin of lying to the Holy Spirit today? Well, pretending to be spiritual, when we are not in tune with God, is lying to the Spirit. Pretending that we are heavy givers, when it is not the truth, is lying to the Spirit. Giving a public testimony for the purpose of impressing the church is lying to the Spirit. Public praying that is done for show is also lying to the Spirit. In fact, any kind of sham or make believe in spiritual matters is lying to the Holy Spirit of God.

The Word of God implies that there are three kinds of religious people who make God sick: (1) The Christian who treats his relationship to Christ halfheartedly (Rev. 3:16); (2) The person who displays an "I am holier than thou" attitude (Isa. 65:5); and (3) the religious hypocrite (Isa. 1:13-14). The sin of Ananias and Sapphira was that of spiritual hypocrisy.

The Holy Spirit is the Spirit of Truth. He hates lying, and lying in spiritual matters is especially obnoxious to Him.

While meditating upon the seriousness of the possibility of lying to the Holy Spirit, we are led to pray with the Psalmist: "If thou, Lord, shouldest mark iniquities, O Lord, who shall stand? But there is forgiveness with thee, that thou mayest be feared" (Ps. 130:3-4). Knowing that the devil likes to get in our thoughts (even while we are in church), let us strive to be honest in our relationships and commitments toward the Body of Christ.

II. The Sin of Grieving the Holy Spirit

"And grieve not the holy Spirit of God, whereby ye are sealed unto the day of redemption" (Eph. 4:30). "How oft did they provoke him in the wilderness, and *grieve him* in the desert!" (Ps. 78:40). "They rebelled, and *vexed* his holy Spirit . . . ." (Isa. 63:10).

The Holy Spirit can be grieved. This fact not only demonstrates that He is a real person, it also implies that He loves God's people very much. To grieve Him means to cause Him real sorrow, which is a form of pain. Strangers cannot deeply grieve us. But the more we love someone, the deeper the hurt when that loved one disappoints us.

The Holy Spirit loves each member of the Body of Christ and is greatly concerned about the spiritual growth and well-being of each member. Because of this love and this concern, He can be grieved. He indwells the believer and therefore is witness to every action, hears every word, and knows every thought. And because the Holy Spirit is *holy*, He is very sensitive regarding evil and is grieved when evil is permitted to ruin the believer's testimony and rob him of spiritual joy.

What is it in the believer's life that grieves the Holy Spirit? Doubtless, all sin grieves Him. However, the context of the injunction: "And grieve not the Holy Spirit of God" leads us to believe certain sins are particularly obnoxious to Him. Let us look at the verses which precede, and those which follow the injunction:

A. We grieve the Holy Spirit by corrupt speech. "Let no corrupt communication proceed out of your mouth, but that which is good to the use of edifying, that it may minister grace unto the hearers. And grieve not the holy Spirit of God . . . ." (Eph. 4:29-30). The real meaning of the Greek word (*sapros*), is "putrid," or "rotten."

Of course, we know that the world is filled with that kind of talk. Dirty stories and suggestive remarks are as common as people. There are men and women who can and do make something suggestive out of anything. The reason for such talk is that the thought of it is in the heart and mind of man. Jesus said:

> That which cometh out of the man, that defileth the man. For from within, out of the heart of men, proceed evil thoughts, adulteries, fornications, murders, thefts, covetousness, wickedness, deceit, lasciviousness, an evil eye, blasphemy, pride, foolishness: All these evil things come from within, and *defile* the man (Mark 7:20-23).

Though it is common in the world, shame on the blood-bought child of God who defiles the "temple of the Holy Spirit" with that kind of talk! Such language is totally out of character with the Christian life. When it occurs, it hurts the sensitive Holy Spirit of God. He wants to use these lips to glorify God, to tell of the goodness of the Lord, to tell others of the salvation of the God of heaven, to talk with the Father in prayer. When those lips are used to repeat the rubbish and filthy stories of the unregenerated world, the Holy Spirit shudders and is grieved.

A gang of boys were planning to do something daring, something that would spell trouble if they were caught. One boy said he could not go with them in this thing. The others chided him and the leader said: "You are chicken because you are afraid your old man will hurt you if he finds out, aren't you?" "No," answered the boy, "I am not afraid that my dad will hurt me if he finds out, but I am afraid that I will hurt him." May our attitude be like that toward the blessed Holy Spirit of God! "And grieve not the holy Spirit of God, whereby ye are sealed unto the day of redemption"!

B. The Holy Spirit is grieved by an unchristian attitude toward others. The verse following the injunction not to grieve the Holy Spirit, exhorts: "Let all *bitterness,* and *wrath,* and *anger,* and *clamour,* and *evil speaking,* be put away from you, with all *malice*: And be ye kind one to another, tenderhearted, forgiving one another, even as God for Christ's sake hath forgiven you" (Eph. 4:31-32).

An unforgiving spirit, nursing a hurt, speaking evil of another—these things are as alien to the very spirit of Christianity as a chicken is alien to a body of water. An attitude of bitterness and resentment is the exact opposite of what the Holy Spirit wants to produce in the Christian life. He wants to produce "love, joy, peace, longsuffering, gentleness . . . ." (Gal. 5:22). An unkind spirit grieves the Holy Spirit. When we hurt one another, we hurt the Spirit.

Can a believer harbor an unkind spirit toward other believers? Yes, but not without hurting himself, and not without grieving the Holy Spirit. I once overheard a Christian lady say: "When I get to heaven I hope I will be just a little above her, so I can spit on her." Yes, I really believe she was saved. She believed in the Lord and meant to please Him. But right then she had bitterness in her heart and she put it into words. Some carry bitterness within, though they do not give expression to it in words. But whether expressed or held in, the Holy Spirit is always grieved by an unforgiving attitude.

The worst case of a Christian being robbed by bitterness that I ever witnessed, occurred in Germany. Ministering there while the regular missionary was on furlough, I noticed a young woman in the congregation who always looked miserable and sad. Upon visiting her I discovered that her heart was filled with resentment against the man who had wronged her. She just could not let go of it, even though she knew the Lord wanted her to forgive. Though I showed her what God's Word said, and though I prayed and pleaded with her to ask the Lord to take the bitterness away, she either could not or would not let go of the resentment. She could have had the peace of God and the joy of the Lord, but not until the resentment was yielded to God. She robbed herself and grieved the tender Spirit of God.

To forgive freely is twice blessed. It blesses the one who forgives, and it blesses the one who is forgiven. Oh, that we might be like Joseph who freely forgave those who had sold him into slavery!

C. Murmuring and complaining will grieve the Holy Spirit. This was the case with Israel in the wilderness. "Forty years long was I *grieved* with this generation . . . ." (Ps. 95:10). What was it that grieved Him most? If the frequency with which it is mentioned means anything, then the murmuring of the people was the greatest cause. I counted at least 16 times that this murmuring is mentioned in the books of Exodus, Numbers, and Deuteronomy.

The Lord does not appreciate it when His people, whom He has redeemed, complain in His service. To the priests who were bored with the Lord's service, He said: "Ye said also, Behold, what a weariness is it! and ye have snuffed at it, saith the Lord of hosts . . . ." (Mal. 1:13).

The priests were the appointed servants of God who stood between the Lord and a sinful people. They offered the sacrifices upon the altar, read the Scriptures and taught the people. In short, they were called to lead the people in the way of God. This was a wonderful privilege, a very sacred service. But they got used to it and instead of being a joy and privilege to them, it became a chore to them. In their hearts they said: "What a weariness is it!" The Lord's service was a burden. They complained. They kept on performing, but their hearts were not in it and they had no joy in serving. And of course, the Lord knew exactly what was in their hearts.

Does this ever happen today? Do pastors, missionaries, Bible teachers, Sunday School workers, deacons, youth workers, nursery attendants, choir leaders, church officers, ever get weary of their service? I do not mean, do they get weary *in* the service, for that is natural. But when we get weary of it, and complain, at least in our hearts, and would like to quit, then the Spirit of God is grieved. To such the Spirit says: "For consider him that endured such contradiction of sinners against himself, lest ye be wearied and faint in your minds" (Heb. 12:3).

To be an ambassador of Jesus Christ is the greatest privilege that man can have on earth. How do we treat this privilege? Do we enter into it with joy and perform it with genuine enthusiasm? Or do we gripe and complain? To take the Lord's service lightly or treat it carelessly, or be weary *of* it, grieves the Holy Spirit of God. Of course, it is hard work! Sure, you won't always be appreciated! But our Lord said: "For whosoever will save his life shall lose it: and whosoever will lose his life for my sake shall find it" (Matt. 16:25). To be a blessing to others always costs. The teacher who saves herself will not bless others. The preacher who does not tire himself will soon tire his congregation. Dear Lord, keep us from the sin of grumbling!

III. The Sin of Quenching the Holy Spirit.

"Quench not the Spirit" (I Thess. 5:19).

To "quench" is to put out the fire, to stifle, to smother, to pour cold water on the leading of the Holy Spirit. How does a believer quench the Holy Spirit? The ministry of the Spirit to the believer is manifold. He teaches, guides, convicts, strives, inspires, encourages. His goal is to shape our lives so that the wonderful characteristics of Jesus become living realities in us, as presented in Galatians 5:22-23. When this endeavor is stifled by the resistance of the believer, the Spirit is quenched. In general, the Holy Spirit is quenched by an attitude of resistance or indifference to the will of God. This may take place in a number of ways.

A. If the Spirit leads us to give a testimony for Christ, and

for one reason or another we do not respond to His leading, we have quenched the Spirit.

B. If the Spirit leads us to speak to someone about the Saviour, and we resist that leading, we have quenched the Spirit.

C. Should the Spirit speak to us about a more complete surrender, about giving more time to the Word and to prayer, concerning confessing and forsaking a sin, or laying aside a hindering weight—if we are aware of the Spirit's gentle leading in any way, and then smother that leading, we are quenching the Holy Spirit.

D. It is possible to quench the Spirit in other believers by discouraging their zeal, or belittling their sincere efforts. This is especially true in our contacts with new Christians. J. Oswald Sanders wrote:

> Who does not enjoy the contagious enthusiasm of the new convert, despite blunders he may make? It is tragically possible, however, for older Christians less zealous and more phlegmatic, to quench the divine flame in the glowing heart by contemptuous words or unsympathetic criticism.

> "You should be ashamed of yourself," said an unspiritual elder to an ungifted young man, who, at tremendous cost to himself, had given a stumbling testimony for Christ.

> "I am ashamed of myself," he rejoined, "But I am not ashamed of my Lord."

> The elder came perilously near quenching the Spirit in the heart of that young man.

What are the results of quenching the Holy Spirit? Perhaps we can take a cue from the experience of the children of Israel in the wilderness, who grieved and quenched the Spirit by their complaining and unfaithfulness. Because of their attitude of unresponsiveness to the leading of the Lord, they were required to live the rest of their lives wandering over the dusty desert. They never did enjoy the land of milk and honey which the Lord meant for them to have.

The life of the Christian who repeatedly says no to the

leading of the Spirit will also be a desert experience. It will be a life marked by spiritual defeat and by the absence of joy and peace which the Lord wanted him to have. That Christian will miss the thrill of seeing God working through him. He will never be able to say in a voice choked with awe and thanksgiving: "My cup runneth over." He may even question the reality of spiritual joy and blessings that others speak of as being part of their lives. Yet, these were meant for him!

I shall never forget an experience I had one Saturday in Ohio. We were new in town and wanted to purchase a piano for our daughter who was taking lessons. While talking to the manager of a large department store, I mentioned that I was a minister of the Gospel. With surprising interest, he responded: "Say, I want you to meet my dad, I am sure he would like to talk with you." We walked to the office and I was introduced to the owner of the store who was advanced in years, but still very active. He asked a number of questions about what I believed and preached. Then he broke down and wept. When he had somewhat regained control of himself, he told me this story about himself: "When I was a young man, the Lord called me to preach the Gospel. I was certain of that call and entered college to prepare for the Christian ministry. But there I fell in with a group of young men who had their hearts set on success in the business world. They told me that I could serve the Lord just as well as a Christian businessman. Well, I got carried away with their enthusiasm and switched over to a business course. At first the Spirit spoke to me about it, but I put it out of my mind. I have been very successful in business. I have given many thousands of dollars to support missionaries. But, Preacher, I would gladly give everything that I have if I could be where you are. I heard the Lord's call and I turned a deaf ear to it. I have lived a miserable life because of that decision."

Lord, forgive us for having put the Spirit down, and help us to be sensitive to His leading, so that we may not grieve Him nor quench His fire, in Jesus' name, amen!

Bibliography

Bickersteth, Edward Henry. *The Trinity.* Grand Rapids: Kregel Publications, 1959.

_____. *The Holy Spirit His Person and Work.* Grand Rapids: Kregel Publications, 1959.

Blackwood, Andrew W. Jr. *The Holy Spirit in Your Life.* Grand Rapids: Baker Book House, 1957.

Boyer, James L. *For a World Like Ours, Studies in I Corinthians.* Winona Lake, Indiana: BMH Books, 1971.

Bruner, Frederick Dale. *A Theology of the Holy Spirit.* Grand Rapids: Wm. B. Eerdmans, Publisher, 1970.

Brunk, George R. II, Editor. *Encounter With the Holy Spirit.* Scottdale: Herald Press, 1972.

Carter, Charles Webb. *The Person and Ministry of the Holy Spirit.* Grand Rapids: Baker Book House, 1974.

Cate, B. F. *The Nine Gifts of the Spirit.* Des Plaines, Illinois: Regular Baptist Press, 1956.

Chafer, Lewis Sperry. *He That Is Spiritual.* Grand Rapids: Zondervan Publishing House, 1976.

_____. *Systematic Theology,* Vol. I and Vol. VI. Dallas: Dallas Seminary Press, 1948.

Cramer, Raymond L. *The Master Key.* Los Angeles: Cowman Publications, 1951.

Criswell, W. A. *The Baptism, Filling & Gifts of the Holy Spirit.* Grand Rapids: Zondervan Publishing House, 1973.

Flynn, Leslie B. *19 Gifts of the Spirit.* Wheaton, Illinois: Victor Books, A Division of SP Publications, 1974.

Freeman, C. Wade, Editor. *The Holy Spirit's Ministry.* Grand Rapids: Zondervan Publishing House, 1954.

Frodsham, Stanley Howard. *The Spirit-Filled Life.* Grand Rapids: Wm. B. Eerdmans Publishing Company, 1948.

Gaebelein, Arnold C. *The Acts of the Apostles*. New York: Loizeaux Brothers, 1961.

Gangel, Kenneth O. *You and Your Spiritual Gifts*. Chicago: Moody Press, 1975.

Gardiner, George E. *The Corinthian Catastrophe*. Grand Rapids: Kregel Publications, 1974.

Gordon, A. J. *The Ministry of the Spirit*. Minneapolis: Bethany Fellowship, 1964.

Gutzke, Manford George. *Plain Talk on Acts*. Grand Rapids: Zondervan Publishing House, 1966.

Harrison, Norman B. *His Indwelling Presence*. Chicago: Moody Press, 1928.

Hughes, Albert. *Witnessing With Power*. Grand Rapids: Zondervan Publishing House, 1938.

Hocking, David L. *Spiritual Gifts*. Long Beach, California: Sounds Of Grace Ministries, 1975.

Ironside, H. A. *The Mission of the Spirit*. New York: Loizeaux Brothers.

Koch, Kurt. *The Strife of Tongues*. Grand Rapids: Kregel Publications, 1971.

LaHaye, Tim. *Spirit-Controlled Temperament*. Wheaton, Illinois: Tyndale House Publishers, 1971.

Massee, J. C. *The Holy Spirit in Scripture and Experience*. Cleveland: Union Gospel Press, 1917.

Macaulay, J. C. *Life in the Spirit*. Grand Rapids: Wm. B. Eerdmans Publishing Company, 1955.

_____. *A Devotional Commentary on the Acts of the Apostles*. Grand Rapids: Wm. B. Eerdmans Publishing Company, 1951.

Morgan, G. Campbell. *The Corinthian Letters of Paul*. New York: Fleming H. Revell Company, 1946.

_____. *The Spirit of God*. New York: Fleming H. Revell Company, 1900.

_____. *The Teaching of Christ*. New York: Fleming H. Revell Company, 1913.

Ockenga, Harold J. *The Spirit of the Living God*. New York: Fleming H. Revell Company, 1947.

Owen, John. *The Holy Spirit, His Gifts and Power*. Evansville, Indiana: Sovereign Grace Publishers, Reprint 1960.

Pache, Réne. *The Person and Work of the Holy Spirit*. Chicago: Moody Press, 1954.

Palmer, Edwin H. *The Holy Spirit.* Nutley, New Jersey: Presbyterian and Reformed Publishing Company, 1973.

Pentecost, J. Dwight. *The Divine Comforter.* Chicago: Moody Press, 1975.

Pierce, Earle V. *Ye Are My Witnesses.* Philadelphia: The Judson Press, 1954.

Rice, John R. *The Power of Pentecost.* Wheaton, Illinois: Sword of the Lord Publishers, 1949.

Ridout, Samuel. *The Person and Work of the Holy Spirit.* New York: Loizeaux Brothers, 1954.

Ryrie, Charles Caldwell. *The Holy Spirit.* Chicago: Moody Press, 1976.

Sanders, J. Oswald. *The Holy Spirit and His Gifts.* Grand Rapids: Zondervan Publishing House, 1974.

Smeaton, George. *The Doctrine of the Holy Spirit.* Edinburgh: The Banner of Truth Trust, 1974.

Smith, Charles R. *Tongues in Biblical Perspective.* Winona Lake, Indiana: BMH Books, 1973.

Unger, Merrill F. *The Baptism and Gifts of the Holy Spirit.* Chicago: Moody Press, 1976.

_____. *New Testament Teaching on Tongues.* Grand Rapids: Kregel Publications, 1974.

Van Ryn, August. *Acts of the Apostles.* New York: Loizeaux Brothers, 1961.

Walvoord, John F. *The Holy Spirit.* Grand Rapids: Zondervan Publishing House, 1974.